Relational Aesthetics

Nicolas Bourriaud
Relational Aesthetics

Translated by Simon Pleasance & Fronza Woods
with the participation of Mathieu Copeland

les presses du réel

Collection Documents sur l'art:

Available in french:
Nicolas Bourriaud, *Esthétique relationnelle*, 1998
Éric Troncy, *Le Colonel Moutarde dans la bibliothèque avec le chandelier*, 1998
Dan Graham, *Rock/Music Textes*, 1999
Robert Nickas, *Vivre libre ou mourir*, 2000
Philippe Parreno, *Speech Bubbles*, 2001
Prières américaines, 2002

Avalaible in english:
Robert Nickas, *Live Free or Die*, 2000
Nicolas Bourriaud, *Relational Aesthetics*, 2002

Foreword

Where do the misunderstandings surrounding 1990s' art come from, if not a theoretical discourse complete with shortcomings? An overwhelming majority of critics and philosophers are reluctant to come to grips with contemporary practices. So these remain essentially unreadable, as their originality and their relevance cannot be perceived by analysing them on the basis of problems either solved or unresolved by previous generations. The oh-so-painful fact has to be accepted that certain issues are no longer being raised, and it is, by extension, important to identify those that are being raised these days by artists. What are the real challenges of contemporary art? What are its links with society, history, and culture? The critic's primary task is to recreate the complex set of problems that arise in a particular period or age, and take a close look at the various answers given. Too often, people are happy drawing up an inventory of yesterday's concerns, the better to lament the fact of not getting any answers. But the very first question, as far as these new approaches are concerned, obviously has to do with the material form of these works. How are these apparently elusive works to be decoded, be they *process-related* or behavioural by ceasing to take shelter behind the sixties art history?

Let us quote several examples of these activities. Rirkrit Tiravanija organises a dinner in a collector's home, and leaves him all the ingredients required to make a Thaï soup. Philippe Parreno invites a few people to pursue their favourite hobbies on May Day, on a factory assembly line. Vanessa Beecroft dresses some twenty women in the same way, complete with a red wig, and the visitor merely gets a glimpse of them through the doorway. Maurizio Cattelan feeds rats on "Bel paese" cheese and sells them as multiples, or exhibits recently robbed safes. In a Copenhagen square, Jes Brinch and Henrik Plenge Jacobsen install an upturned bus that causes a rival riot in the city. Christine Hill works as a check-out assistant in a supermarket, organises a weekly gym workshop in a gallery. Carsten Höller recreates the chemical formula of molecules secreted by the human brain when in love, builds an inflatable plastic yacht, and breeds chaffinches with the aim of teaching them a new song. Noritoshi Hirakawa puts a small ad in a newspaper to find a girl to take part in his show. Pierre Huyghe summons people to a casting session, makes a TV transmitter available to the public, and puts a photograph of labourers at work on view just a few yards from the building site. One could add many other names and works to such a list. Anyhow, the liveliest factor that is played out on the chessboard of art has to do with interactive, user-friendly and relational concepts.

These days, communications are plunging human contacts into monitored areas that divide the social bond up into (quite) different products. Artistic activity, for its part, strives to achieve modest connections, open up (One or two) obstructed passages, and connect levels of reality kept apart from one another. The much vaunted "communication superhighways", with their toll plazas and picnic areas, threaten to become the only possible thoroughfare from a point to another in the human world. The superhighway may well actually help us to travel faster and more efficiently, yet it has the drawback of turning its users into consumers of miles and their by-products. We feel meagre and helpless when faced with the electronic media, theme parks, user-friendly places, and the spread of compatible forms of sociability, like the laboratory rat doomed to an inexorable itinerary in its cage, littered with chunks of cheese.

The ideal subject of the society of extras is thus reduced to the condition of a consumer of time and space.

For anything that cannot be marketed will inevitably vanish. Before long, it will not be possible to maintain relationships between people outside these trading areas. So here we are summonsed to talk about things around a duly priced drink, as a symbolic form of contemporary human relations. You are looking for shared warmth, and the comforting feeling of well being for two? So try our coffee… The space of current relations is thus the space most severely affected by general reification. The relationship between people, as symbolised by goods or replaced by them, and signposted by logos, has to take on extreme and clandestine forms, if it is to dodge the empire of predictability. The social bond has turned into a standardised artefact. In a world governed by the division of labour and ultra-specialisation, mechanisation and the law of profitability, it behoves the powers that human relations should be channelled towards accordingly planned outlets, and that they should be pursued on the basis of one or two simple principles, which can be both monitored and repeated. The supreme "separation", the separation that affects relational channels, represents the final stage in the transformation to the "Society of the Spectacle" as described by Guy Debord. This is a society where human relations are no longer "directly experienced", but start to become blurred in their "spectacular" representation. Herein lies the most burning issue to do with art today: is it still possible to generate relationships with the world, in a practical field art-history traditionally earmarked for their "representation"? Contrary to what Debord thought, for all he saw in the art world was a reservoir of examples of what had to be tangibly "achieved" in day-to-day life, artistic praxis appears these days to be a rich loam for social experiments, like a space partly protected from the uniformity of behavioural patterns. The works we shall be discussing here outline so many hands-on utopias.

Some of the following essays were originally published in magazines –for the most part in *Documents sur l'art*, and exhibition catalogues[1], but have been considerably reworked, not to say re-ordered, here. Others are previously unpublished. This collection of essays is also rounded off by a glossary, which readers may refer to whenever a problematic concept rears its head. To make the book that much easier to come to grips with, may we suggest to turn right away to the definition of the word "Art".

1. "Le paradigme esthétique (Félix Guattari et L'art)" was published by the magazine *Chimères*, 1993; "Relation écran" was published in the catalogue for the 3rd Lyon Contemporary Art Biennial, 1995.

Relational form

Artistic activity is a game, whose forms, patterns and functions develop and evolve according to periods and social contexts; it is not an immutable essence. It is the critic's task to study this activity in the present. A certain aspect of the programme of modernity has been fairly and squarely wound up (and not, let us hasten to emphasise in these bourgeois times, the spirit informing it). This completion has drained the criteria of aesthetic judgement we are heir to of their substance, but we go on applying them to present-day artistic practices. The *new* is no longer a criterion, except among latter-day detractors of modern art who, where the much-execrated present is concerned, cling solely to the things that their traditionalist culture has taught them to loathe in yesterday's art. In order to invent more effective tools and more valid viewpoints, it behoves us to understand the changes nowadays occurring in the social arena, and grasp what has already changed and what is still changing. How are we to understand the types of artistic behaviour shown in exhibitions held in the 1990s, and the lines of thinking behind them, if we do not start out from the same *situation* as the artists?

Contemporary artistic practice and its cultural plan
The modern political era, which came into being with the Enlightenment, was based on the desire to emancipate individuals and people. The advances of technologies and freedoms, the

decline of ignorance, and improved working conditions were all billed to free humankind and help to usher in a better society. There are several versions of modernity, however. The 20th century was thus the arena for a struggle between two visions of the world: a modest, rationalist conception, hailing from the 18th century, and a philosophy of spontaneity and liberation through the irrational (Dada, Surrealism, the Situationists), both of which were opposed to authoritarian and utilitarian forces eager to gauge human relations and subjugate people. Instead of culminating in hoped-for emancipation, the advances of technologies and "Reason" made it that much easier to exploit the South of planet earth, blindly replace human labour by machines, and set up more and more sophisticated subjugation techniques, all through a general rationalisation of the production process. So the modern emancipation plan has been substituted by countless forms of melancholy.

Twentieth century avant-garde, from Dadaism to the Situationist International, fell within the tradition of this modern project (changing culture, attitudes and mentalities, and individual and social living conditions), but it is as well to bear in mind that this project was already there before them, differing from their plan in many ways. For modernity cannot be reduced to a rationalist teleology, any more than it can to political messianism. Is it possible to disparage the desire to improve living and working conditions, on the pretext of the bankruptcy of tangible attempts to do as much-shored up by totalitarian ideologies and naïve visions of history? What used to be called the avant-garde has, needless to say, developed from the ideological swing of things offered by modern rationalism; but it is now re-formed on the basis of quite different philosophical, cultural and social presuppositions. It is evident that today's art is carrying on this fight, by coming up with perceptive, experimental, critical and participatory models, veering in the direction indicated by Enlightenment philosophers, Proudhon, Marx, the Dadaists and Mondrian. If opinion is striving to acknowledge the legitimacy and interest of these experiments, this is because they are no longer presented like the precursory phenomena of an inevitable historical evolution. Quite to the contrary, they appear fragmentary and isolated, like orphans of an overall view of the world bolstering them with the clout of an ideology.

It is not modernity that is dead, but its idealistic and teleological version.

Today's fight for modernity is being waged in the same terms as yesterday's, barring the fact that the avant-garde has stopped patrolling like some scout, the troop having come to a cautious standstill around a bivouac of certainties. Art was intended to prepare and announce a future world: today it is modelling possible universes.

The ambition of artists who include their practice within the slipstream of historical modernity is to repeat neither its forms nor its claims, and even less assign to art the same functions as it. Their task is akin to the one that Jean-François Lyotard allocated to post-modern architecture, which "*is condemned to create a series of minor modifications in a space whose modernity it inherits, and abandon an overall reconstruction of the space inhabited by humankind*[1]". What is more, Lyotard seems to half-bemoan this state of affairs: he defines it negatively, by using the term "condemned". And what, on the other hand, if this "condemnation" represented the historical chance whereby most of the art worlds known to us managed to spread their wings, over the past ten years or so? This "chance" can be summed up in just a few words: *learning to inhabit the world in a better way*, instead of trying to construct it based on a preconceived idea of historical evolution. Otherwise put, the role of artworks is no longer to form imaginary and utopian realties, but to actually be ways of living and models of action within the existing real, whatever the scale chosen by the artist. Althusser said that one always catches the world's train on the move; Deleuze, that "grass grows from the middle" and not from the bottom or the top. The artist dwells in the circumstances the present offers him, so as to turn the setting of his life (his links with the physical and conceptual world) into a lasting world. He catches the world on the move: he is a *tenant of culture*, to borrow Michel de Certeau's expression[2]. Nowadays, modernity extends into the practices of cultural do-it-yourself and recycling, into the invention of the everyday and the development of time lived, which are not objects less deserving of attention and examination than Messianistic utopias and the formal "novelties" that typified modernity yesterday. There is nothing more absurd either than the assertion that contemporary art does not involve any political project, or than the claim that its subversive aspects are not based on any theoretical terrain. Its plan, which has just as much to do with working conditions and the conditions in which cultural objects are produced, as with the changing forms of social life, may nevertheless seem dull to minds formed in the mould of cultural Darwinism. Here, then, is the time of the "dolce utopia", to use Maurizio Cattelan's phrase...

Artwork as social interstice

The possibility of a *relational* art (an art taking as its theoretical horizon the realm of human interactions and its social context, rather than the assertion of an independent and *private* symbolic space), points to a radical upheaval of the aesthetic, cultural and political goals introduced by modern art. To sketch a sociology of this, this evolution stems essentially from the birth of a world-wide urban culture, and from the extension of this city model to more or less all cultural phenomena. The general growth of towns and cities, which took off at the end of the Second World War, gave rise not only to an extraordinary upsurge of social exchanges, but also to much greater individual mobility (through the development of networks and roads, and telecommunications, and the gradual freeing-up of isolated places, going with the opening-up of attitudes). Because of the crampedness of dwelling spaces in this urban world, there was, in tandem, a scaling-down of furniture and objects, now emphasising a greater manoeuvrability. If, for a long period of time, the artwork has managed to come across as a luxury, lordly item in this urban setting (the dimensions of the work, as well as those of the apartment, helping to distinguish between their owner and the crowd), the development of the function of artworks and the way they are shown attest to a growing *urbanisation* of the artistic experiment. What is collapsing before our very eyes is nothing other than this falsely aristocratic conception of the arrangement of works of art, associated with the feeling of territorial acquisition. In other words, it is no longer possible to regard the contemporary work as a space to be walked through (the "owner's tour" is akin to the collector's). It is henceforth presented as a period of time to be lived through, like an opening to unlimited discussion. The city has ushered in and spread the hands-on experience: it is the tangible symbol and historical setting of the state of society, that *"state of encounter imposed on people"*, to use Althusser's expression[3], contrasting with that dense and "trouble-free" jungle which the *natural state* once was, according to Jean-Jacques Rousseau, a jungle hampering any lasting encounter. Once raised to the power of an absolute rule of civilisation, this system of intensive encounters has ended up producing linked artistic practices: an art form where the substrate is formed by inter-subjectivity, and which takes being-together as a central theme, the "encounter" between beholder and picture, and the collective elaboration of meaning. Let us leave the matter of the historicity of this phenomenon on one side: art has always been relational in varying degrees, i.e. a factor of sociability and a founding principle of dialogue. One of the virtual properties of the image is its power of *linkage* (Fr. *reliance),* to borrow Michel Maffesoli's term: flags, logos, icons, signs, all produce empathy and sharing, and all generate *bond*[4]. Art (practices stemming from painting and sculpture which come across in the form of an exhibition) turns out to be particularly suitable when it comes to expressing this hands-on civilisation, because it *tightens the space of relations*, unlike TV and literature which refer each individual person to his or her space of private consumption, and also unlike theatre and cinema which bring small groups together before specific, unmistakable images. Actually, there is no live comment made about what is seen (the discussion time is put off until after the show). At an exhibition, on the other hand, even when inert forms are involved, there is the possibility of an immediate discussion, in both senses of the term. I see and perceive, I comment, and I evolve in a unique space and time. Art is the place that produces a specific sociability. It remains to be seen what the status of this is in the set of "states of encounter" proposed by the City. How is an art focused on the production of such forms of conviviality capable of re-launching the modern emancipation plan, by complementing it? How does it permit the development of new politicaland cultural designs?

Before giving concrete examples, it is well worth reconsidering the place of artworks in the overall economic system, be it symbolic or material, which governs contemporary society. Over and above its mercantile nature and its semantic value, the work of art represents a social *interstice*. This *interstice* term was used by Karl Marx to describe trading communities that elude the capitalist economic context by being removed from the law of profit: barter, merchandising, autarkic types of production, etc. The interstice is a space in human relations which fits more or less harmoniously and openly into the overall system, but suggests other trading possibilities than those in effect within this system. This is the precise nature of the contemporary art exhibition in the arena of representational commerce: it creates free areas, and time spans whose rhythm contrasts with those structuring everyday life, and it encourages an inter-human commerce that differs from the "communication zones" that are imposed upon us. The present-day social context restricts the possibilities of inter-human relations all the more because it creates spaces planned to this end. Automatic public toilets were invented to keep streets clean. The same spirit underpins the development of communication tools, while city streets are swept clean of all manners of relational dross, and neighbourhood relationships fizzle. The general mechanisation of social functions gradually reduces the relational space. Just a few years ago, the telephone wake-up call service employed human beings, but now we are woken up by a synthesised voice... The automatic cash machine has become the transit model for the most elementary of social functions, and professional behaviour patterns are modelled on the efficiency of the machines replacing them, these machines carrying out tasks which once represented so many opportunities for exchanges, pleasure and squabbling. Contemporary art is definitely developing a political project when it endeavours to move into the relational realm by turning it into an issue.

When Gabriel Orozco puts an orange on the stalls of a deserted Brazilian market (*Crazy Tourist*, 1991), or slings a hammock in the MoMA garden in New York (*Hamoc en la moma*, 1993), he is operating at the hub of "social infra-thinness" (l'inframince social), that minute space of daily gestures determined by the superstructure made up of "big" exchanges, and defined by it. Without any wording, Orozco's photographs are a documentary record of tiny revolutions in the common urban and semi-urban life (a sleeping bag on the grass, an empty shoebox, etc.). They record this silent, still life nowadays formed by relationships with the other. When Jens Haaning broadcasts funny stories in Turkish through a loudspeaker in a Copenhagen square (*Turkish Jokes*, 1994), he produces in that split second a micro-community, one made up of immigrants brought together by collective laughter which upsets their exile situation, formed in relation to the work and in it. The exhibition is the special place where such momentary groupings may occur, governed as they are by differing principles. And depending on the degree of participation required of the onlooker by the artist, along with the nature of the works and the models of sociability proposed and represented, an exhibition will give rise to a specific "arena of exchange". And this "arena of exchange", must be judged on the basis of aesthetic criteria, in other words, by analysing the coherence of its form, and then the symbolic value of the "world" it suggests to us, and of the image of human relations reflected by it. Within this social interstice, the artist must assume the symbolic models he shows. All representation (though contemporary art *models* more than it represents, and fits into the social fabric more than it draws inspiration therefrom) refers to values that can be transposed into society. As a human activity based on commerce, art is at once the object and the subject of an ethic. And this all the more so because, unlike other activities, *its sole function is to be exposed to this commerce.*

Art is a state of encounter.

Relational aesthetics and random materialism

Relational aesthetics is part of a materialistic tradition. Being "materialistic" does not mean sticking to the triteness of facts, nor does it imply that sort of narrow-mindedness that consists in reading works in purely economic terms. The philosophical tradition that underpins this *relational aesthetics* was defined in a noteworthy way by Louis Althusser, in one of his last writings, as a "materialism of encounter", or random materialism. This particular materialism takes as its point of departure the world contingency, which has no pre-existing origin or sense, nor Reason, which might allot it a purpose. So the essence of humankind is purely trans-individual, made up of bonds that link individuals together in social forms which are invariably historical (Marx: the human essence is the set of social relations). There is no such thing as any possible "end of history" or "end of art", because the game is being forever re-enacted, in relation to its function, in other words, in relation to the players and the system which they construct and criticise. Hubert Damisch saw in the "end of art" theories the outcome of an irksome muddle between the "end of the game" and the "end of play". A new game is announced as soon as the social setting radically changes, without the meaning of the game itself being challenged[5]. This *inter-human game* which forms our object (Duchamp: "*Art is a game between all people of all periods*") nevertheless goes beyond the context of what is called "art" by commodity. So the "constructed situations" advocated by the Situationist International belong in their own right to this "game", in spite of Guy Debord who, in the final analysis, denied them any artistic character. For in them, quite to the contrary, he saw "art being exceeded" by a revolution in day-to-day life. Relational aesthetics does not represent a theory of art, this would imply the statement of an origin and a destination, but a theory of form.

What do we mean by *form*? A coherent unit, a structure (*independent entity of inner dependencies*) which shows the typical features of a world. The artwork does not have an exclusive hold on it, it is merely a subset in the overall series of existing forms. In the materialistic philosophical tradition ushered in by Epicurus and Lucretius, atoms fall in parallel formations into the void, following a slightly diagonal course. If one of these atoms swerves off course, it "*causes an encounter with the next atom and from encounter to encounter a pile-up, and the birth of the world*"... This is how forms come into being, from the "deviation" and random encounter between two hitherto parallel elements. In order to create a world, this encounter must be a *lasting* one: the elements forming it must be joined together in a form, in other words, there must have been "*a setting of elements on one another (the way ice 'sets')*". "Form can be defined as a lasting encounter". Lasting encounters, lines and colours inscribed on the surface of a Delacroix painting, the scrap objects that litter Schwitters' "Merz pictures", Chris Burden's performances: over and above the quality of the page layout or the spatial layout, they turn out to be *lasting* from the moment when their components form a whole whose sense "holds good" at the moment of their birth, stirring up new "possibilities of life". All works, down to the most critical and challenging of projects, passes through this viable world state, because they get elements held apart to *meet:* for example, death and the media in Andy Warhol. Deleuze and Guattari were not saying anything different when they defined the work of art as a "block of affects and percepts". Art *keeps together* moments of subjectivity associated with singular experiences, be it Cézanne's apples or Buren's striped structures. The composition of this *bonding agent*, whereby encountering atoms manage to form a word, is, needless to say, dependent on the historical context. What today's informed public understands by "keeping together" is not the same thing that this public imagined back in the 19th century. Today, the "glue" is less obvious, as our visual experience has become more complex, enriched by a century of photographic images, then cinematography (introduction of the sequence shot as a new dynamic unity), enabling us to recognise as a "world" a collection of disparate element (installation, for instance) that no unifying matter, no bronze, links. Other technologies may allow the human spirit to recognise other types of "world-forms" still unknown: for example, computer science put forward the notion of program, that inflect the approach of some artist's way of working. An artist's artwork thus acquires the status of an ensemble of units to be re-activated by the beholder-manipulator. I want to insist on the instability and the diversity of the concept of "form", notion whose outspread can be witnessed in injunction by the founder of sociology, Emile Durckheim, considering the "social fact" as a "thing"… As the artistic "thing" sometime offers itself as a "fact" or an ensemble of facts that happens in the time or space, and whose unity (making it a form, a world) can not be questioned. The setting is widening; after the isolated object, it now can embrace the whole scene: the form of Gordon Matta-Clark or Dan Graham's work can not be reduced to the "things" those two artist "produce"; it is not the simple secondary effects of a composition, as the formalistic aesthetic would like to advance, but the principle acting as a trajectory evolving through signs, objects, forms, gestures… The contemporary artwork's form is spreading out from its material form: it is a linking element, a principle of dynamic agglutination. An artwork is a dot on a line.

Form and others' gaze

If, as Serge Daney writes, *"all form is a face looking at us"*, what does a form become when it is plunged into the dimension of dialogue? What is a form that is essentially *relational*? It seems worth while to discuss this question by taking Daney's formula as a point of reference, precisely because of its ambivalence: as forms are looking at us, how are we to look at them?

Form is most often defined as an outline contrasting with a content. But modernist aesthetics talks about "formal beauty" by referring to a sort of (con)fusion between style and content, and an inventive compatibility of the former with the latter. We judge a work through its plastic or visual form. The most common criticism to do with new artistic practices consists, moreover, in denying them any "formal effectiveness", or in singling out their shortcomings in the "formal resolution". In observing contemporary artistic practices, we ought to talk of "formations" rather than "forms". Unlike an object that is closed in on itself by the intervention of a style and a signature, present-day art shows that form only exists in the encounter and in the dynamic relationship enjoyed by an artistic proposition with other formations, artistic or otherwise.

There are no forms in nature, in the wild state, as it is our gaze that creates these, by cutting them out in the depth of the visible. Forms are *developed,* one from another. What was yesterday regarded as formless or "informal" is no longer these things today. When the aesthetic discussion evolves, the status of form evolves along with it, and through it.

In the novels of polish writer Witold Gombrowicz, we see how each individual generates his own *form* through his behaviour, his way of coming across, and the way he addresses others. This form comes about in the borderline area where the individual struggles with the Other, so as to subject him to what he deems to be his "being". So, for Gombrowicz, our "form" is merely a relational property, linking us with those who reify us by the way they see us, to borrow a Sartrian terminology. When the individual thinks he is casting an objective eye upon himself, he is, in the final analysis, contemplating nothing other than the result of perpetual transactions with the subjectivity of others.

The artistic form, for some, side-steps this inevitability, for it is publicised by a *work*. Our persuasion, conversely, is that form only assumes its texture (and only acquires a real existence) when it introduces human interactions. The form of an artwork issues from a negotiation with the intelligible, which is bequeathed to us. Through it, the artist embarks upon a dialogue. The artistic practice thus resides in the invention of relations between consciousness. Each particular artwork is a proposal to live in a shared world, and the work of every artist is a bundle of relations with the world, giving rise to other relations, and so on and so forth, ad infinitum.

Here we are at the opposite end of this authoritarian version of art which we discover in the essays of Thierry de Duve[6], for whom any work is nothing other than a "sum of judgements", both historical and aesthetic, stated by the artist in the act of its production. To paint is to become part of history through plastic and visual choices. We are in the presence of a prosecutor's aesthetics, here, for which the artist confronts the history of art in the autarky of his own persuasions. It is an aesthetics that reduces artistic practice to the level of a pettifogging historical criticism. Practical "judgement", thus aimed, is peremptory and final in each instance, hence the negation of dialogue, which, alone, grants form a productive status: the status of an "encounter". As part of a "relationist" theory of art, inter-subjectivity does not only represent the social setting for the reception of art, which is its "environment", its "field" (Bourdieu), but also becomes the quintessence of artistic practice.

As Daney suggested, form becomes "face" through the effect of this invention of relations. This formula, needless to add, calls to mind the one acting as the pedestal for Emmanuel Lévinas' thinking, for whom the face represents the sign of the ethical taboo. The face, Lévinas asserts, is *"what orders me to serve another"*, *"what forbids me to kill"*[7]. Any "inter-subjective relation" proceeds by way of the form of the face, which symbolises the responsibility we have towards others: *"the bond with others is only made as responsibility"*, he writes, but don't ethics have a horizon other than this humanism which reduces inter-subjectivity to a kind of inter-servility? Is the image, which, for Daney, is a metaphor of the face, only therefore suitable for producing taboos and proscriptions, through the burden of "responsibility"? When Daney explains that *"all form is a face looking at us"*, he does not merely mean that we are responsible for this. To be persuaded of as much, suffice it to revert to the profound significance of the image for Daney. For him, the image is not "immoral" when it puts us "in the place where we were not"[8], when it "takes the place of another". What is involved here, for Daney, is not solely a reference to the aesthetics of Bazin and Rossellini, claiming the "ontological realism" of the cinematographic art, which even if it does lie at the origin of Daney's thought, does not sum it up. He maintains that form, in an image, is nothing other than the representation of desire. Producing a form is to invent possible encounters; receiving a form is to create the conditions for an exchange, the way you return a service in a game of tennis. If we nudge Daney's reasoning a bit further, form is the *representative* of desire in the image. It is the horizon based on which the image may have a meaning, by pointing to a desired world, which the beholder thus becomes capable of discussing, and based on which his own desire can rebound. This exchange can be summed up by a binomial: someone shows something to someone who returns it as he sees fit. The work tries to catch my gaze, the way the new-born child "asks for" its mother's gaze. In *La Vie commune*, Tzvetan Todorov has shown how the essence of sociability is the need for acknowledgement, much more than competition and violence[9]. When an artist shows us something, he uses a transitive ethic which places his work between the "look-at-me" and the "look-at-that". Daney's most recent writings lament the end of this "Show/See" pairing, which represented the essence of a democracy of the image in favour of another pairing, this one TV-related and authoritarian, "Promote/receive", marking the advent of the "Visual". In Daney's thinking, *"all form is a face looking at me"*, because it is summoning me to dialogue with it. Form is a dynamic that is included both, or turn by turn, in time and space. Form can only come about from a meeting between two levels of reality. For homogeneity does not produce images: it produces the visual, otherwise put, "looped information".

1. Jean-François Lyotard: *"The post modern explained to children"*, London, Turnaround, 1992.
2. Michel de Certeau: *Manières de faire*, Editions Idées-Gallimard.
3. Louis Althusser: *Ecrits philosophiques et politiques*, Editions Stock-IMEC, 1995, p. 557.
4. Michel Maffesoli: *La contemplation du monde*, Editions Grasset, 1993.
5. Hubert Damisch: *Fenêtre jaune cadmium*, Editions du Seuil.
6. Thierry de Duve: *Essais datés*. Editions de La Différence, 1987.
7. Emmanuel Lévinas: *Ethique et infini*, Poche-Biblio, p. 93.
8. Serge Daney: *Persévérance*, Editions P.O.L., 1992, p. 38.
9. Tzvetan Todorov: *La Vie commune*, Editions du Seuil, 1994.

Art of the 1990s

Participation and transitivity

A metal gondola encloses a gas ring that is lit, keeping a large bowl of water on the boil. Camping gears is scattered around the gondola in no particular order. Stacked against the wall are cardboard boxes, most of them open, containing dehydrated Chinese soups which visitors are free to add the boiling water to and eat.

This piece, by Rirkrit Tiravanija, produced for the *Aperto* 93 at the Venice Biennial, remains around the edge of any definition: is it a sculpture? an installation? a performance? an example of social activism? In the last few years, pieces such as this have increased considerably. In international exhibitions we have seen a growing number of stands offering a range of services, works proposing a precise contract to viewers, and more or less tangible models of sociability. Spectator "participation", theorised by Fluxus happenings and performances, has become a constant feature of artistic practice. As for the space of reflection opened up by Marcel Duchamp's "art coefficient", attempting to create precise boundaries for the receiver's field of activity in the artwork, this is nowadays being resolved in a culture of interactivity which posits the transitivity of the cultural object as a fait accompli. As such, these factors merely ratify a development that goes way beyond the mere realm of art. The share of interactivity grows in volume within the set of communication vehicles. On the other hand, the emergence of new technologies, like the Internet and multimedia systems, points to a collective desire to create new areas of conviviality and introduce new types of transaction with regard to the cultural object. The "society of the spectacle" is thus followed by the society of extras, where everyone finds the illusion of an interactive democracy in more or less truncated channels of communication...

Transitivity is as old as the hills. It is a tangible property of the artwork. Without it, the work is nothing other than a dead object, crushed by contemplation. Delacroix wrote in his diary that a successful picture temporarily "condensed" an emotion that it was the duty of the beholder's eye to bring to life and develop. This idea of transitivity introduces into the aesthetic arena that formal disorder which is inherent to dialogue. It denies the existence of any specific "place of art", in favour of a forever unfinished discursiveness, and a never recaptured desire for dissemination. It is against this closed conception of artistic practice, incidentally, that Jean-Luc Godard rebelled against, when he explained that *it takes two to make an image*. This proposition may well seem to borrow Duchamp's, putting forward the notion that *it's the beholder who make pictures*, but it actually takes things a step further by postulating dialogue as the actual origin of the image-making process. At the outset of this, negotiations have to be undertaken, and the Other presupposed... Any artwork might thus be defined as a relational object, like the geometric place of a negotiation with countless correspondents and recipients. It seems possible, in our view, to describe the specific nature of present-day art with the help of the concept of creating relations outside the field of art (in contrast to relations inside it, offering it its socio-economic underlay): relations between individuals and groups, between the artist and the world, and, by way of transitivity, between the beholder and the world. Pierre Bourdieu regards the art world as a *"space of objective relations between positions"*, in other words, a microcosm defined by power plays and struggles whereby producers strive to "preserve or transform it"[1]. Like any other social arena, the art world is essentially relational, insofar as it presents a "*system of differential positions*" through which it can be read. There are many ways of stating this "relational" reading. As part of their networking works, the Ramo Nash Club (Devautour collection artists) thus suggests that "*art is an extremely co-operative system. The dense network of interconnections between members means that everything that happens in it will possibly be a function of all members*". Which gives them a chance to assert that "*it's art that makes art, not artists*". These latter are thus mere unwitting instruments in the service of laws that exceed them, like Napoleon or Alexander the Great in Tolstoy's Theory of History... I don't go along with this cyber-deterministic position, for if the inner structure of the art world actually outlines a limited set of "Possible", this structure relies on a second order of external relations, producing and legitimising the order of internal relations. In a word, the "Art" network is porous, and it is the relations of this network with all the areas of production that determines its development. It would be possible, furthermore, to write a history of art that is the history of this production of relations with the world, by naïvely raising the issue of the nature of the external relations "invented" by artworks.

To give a broad historical picture, let us say that artworks were first situated in a transcendent world, within which art aimed at introducing ways of communicating with the deity. It acted as an interface between human society and the invisible forces governing its movements, alongside a nature that represented the model order. An understanding of this order made it possible to draw closer to divine designs. Art gradually abandoned this goal, and explored the relations existing between Man and the world. This new, relational, dialectical order developed from the Renaissance on, a period that attached great importance to the physical situation of the human being in his world, even if this world was still ruled by the divine figure, with the help of new visual tools such as Alberti's perspective, anatomical realism, and Leonardo da Vinci's "Sfumato". This artwork's purpose was not radically challenged until the arrival of Cubism which attempted to analyse our visual links with the world by way of the most nondescript everyday objects and features (the corner of a table, pipes and guitars), based on a mental realism that reinstated the moving mechanisms of our acquaintance with the object.

The relational arena opened up by the Italian Renaissance was thus gradually applied to more and more limited objects. The question: "What is our relationship to the physical world?" had a bearing, first and foremost, on the entirety of the real, then on limited parts of this same reality. Needless to say, this is in no way a linear progression. One finds painters like Seurat, the rigorous analyst of our ocular ways of perception, living at the same time as someone like Odilon Redon, who tried to see through our relations with the invisible. Essentially, though, the history of art can be read like the history of successive external relational fields, propped up by practices determined by the internal development of these fields. It is the history of the production of relations with the world, as publicised by a class of objects and specific practices.

Today, this history seems to have taken a new turn. After the area of relations between Humankind and deity, and then between Humankind and the object, artistic practice is now focused upon the sphere of inter-human relations, as illustrated by artistic activities that have been in progress since the early 1990s. So the artist sets his sights more and more clearly on the relations that his work will create among his public, and on the invention of models of sociability. This specific production determines not only an ideological and practical arena, but new formal fields as well. By this, I mean that over and above the relational character intrinsic to the artwork, the figures of reference of the sphere of human relations have now become fully-fledged artistic "forms". Meetings, encounters, events, various types of collaboration between people, games, festivals, and places of conviviality, in a word all manner of encounter and relational invention thus represent, today, aesthetic objects likely to be looked at as such, with pictures and sculptures regarded here merely as specific cases of a production of forms with something other than a simple aesthetic consumption in mind.

Typology

Connections and meetings

Pictures and sculptures are characterised, by their symbolic availability. Beyond obvious material impossibilities (museum closing times, geographical remoteness), an artwork can be see at any time. It is there before our eyes, offered to the curiosity of a theoretically universal public. Now, contemporary art is often marked by non-availability, by being viewable only at a specific time. The example of performance is the most classic of all. Once the performance is over, all that remains is documentation that should not be confused with the work itself. This type of activity presupposes a contract with the viewer, an "arrangement" whose clauses have tended to become diversified since the 1960s. The artwork is thus no longer presented to be consumed within a "monumental" time frame and open for a universal public; rather, it elapses within a factual time, for an audience *summoned by* the artist. In a nutshell, the work prompts meetings and invites appointments, managing its own temporal structure. Meetings with a public are not necessarily involved. Marcel Duchamp, for example, invented his "Rendez-vous d'art", by arbitrarily ordaining that, at a certain time of the day, the first object within his reach would be transformed into a readymade. Others have summoned the public to observe a specific phenomenon, the way Robert Barry announced that at "*a certain moment during the morning of the 5th of March 1969, half a cubic metre of helium was released into the atmosphere*" by him. The spectator is thus prompted to move in order to observe a work, which only exists as an artwork by virtue of this observation. In January 1970, Christian Boltanski sent a few acquaintances an SOS letter that was sufficiently vague in its content to be a standard letter, like On Kawara's telegrams informing their addressees, likewise from 1970 onwards, that he was "still alive". Today, the form of the visiting card (used by Dominique Gonzalez-Foerster, Liam Gillick and Jeremy Deller) and the address book (some of Karen Kilimnik's drawings), the growing importance of the opening as part of the exhibition programme (Parreno, Joseph, Tiravanija, Huyghe), together with the originality endeavour made in the production of invitations (hanfover from mail-art), illustrate the importance of this "rendez-vous" represented by the artistic arena, and which forms its relational dimension.

Conviviality and encounters

A work may operate like a relational device containing a certain degree of randomness, or a machine provoking and managing individual and group encounters. To mention just a few examples from the past two decades, this applies to Braco Dimitrijevic's *Casual Passer-by* series, which exaggeratedly celebrate the name and face of an anonymous passer-by on an advertisement-sized poster, or alongside the bust of a celebrity. In the early 1970s, Stephen Willats painstakingly mapped the relationships existing between the inhabitants of an apartment block. And Sophie Calle's work consists largely in describing her meetings with strangers. Whether she is following a passer-by, rummaging through hotel rooms after being employed as a chambermaid, or asking blind people what their definition of beauty is, she formalises, after the fact, a biographical experience which leads her to "collaborate" with the people she meets. Let us further mention, the On Kawara's *I met* series, the *Food* restaurant opened in 1971 by Gordon Matta-Clark, the dinners organized by Daniel Spoerri, and the ludic shop called *La cédille qui sourit* [*The Smiling Cedilla*] opened by George Brecht and Robert Filliou in Villefranche. The constitution of convivial relations has been an historical constant since the 1960s. The generation of the 1990s took up this set of issues, though it had been relieved of the matter of the definition of art, so pivotal in the 1960s and 1970s. The issue no longer resides in broadening the boundaries of art[2], but in experiencing art's capacities of resistance within the overall social arena. Based on one and the same family of activities, two radically different set of problems emerge: yesterday, the stress laid on relations inside the art world, within a modernist culture attaching great importance to the "new" and calling for linguistic subversion; today, the emphasis put on external relations as part of an eclectic culture where the artwork stands up to the mill of the "Society of the Spectacle". Social utopias and revolutionary hopes have given way to everyday micro-utopias and imitative strategies, any stance that is "directly" critical of society is futile, if based on the illusion of a marginality that is nowadays impossible, not to say regressive. Almost thirty years ago, Félix Guattari was advocating those hands-on strategies that underpin present-day artistic practices: "*Just as I think it is illusory to aim at a step-by-step transformation of society, so I think that microscopic attempts, of the community and neighbourhood committee type, the organisation of day-nurseries in the faculty, and the like, play an absolutely crucial role*[3]".

Traditional critical philosophy (the Frankfurt school, in particular) now only fuels art in the form of archaic folklore, a magnificent but ineffectual toy. The subversive and critical function of contemporary art is now achieved in the invention of individual and collective vanishing lines, in those temporary and nomadic constructions whereby the artist models and disseminates disconcerting situations. Whence the present-day craze for revisited areas of conviviality, crucibles where heterogeneous forms of sociability are worked out. For her show at the CCC in Tours, Angela Bulloch set up a café. When a certain number of visitors sat down on the seats, these latter set off the broadcast of a piece of music by Kraftwerk (1993)... For the *Restaurant* exhibition in Paris, in October 1993, Georgina Starr described the anxiety she felt about "having supper on her own", and wrote a text that was handed out to lone diners in the restaurant. Ben Kinmont, for his part, proposed randomly selected people that he would do their washing-up, and kept an information network around his works. On several occasions, Lincoln Tobier has set up a radio station in art galleries, and invited the public to a discussion then broadcast over the airwaves.

Philippe Parreno has been particularly inspired by the notion of party. His exhibition project at Le Consortium in Dijon (January 1995) consisted in *"occupying two hours of time rather than square metres of space"*, which involved organising a party where all the ingredients ended up producing relational forms –clusters of individuals around art objects in situation... Rirkrit Tiravanija, on the other hand, has explored the socio-professional aspect of conviviality, by including in the *Surfaces de réparation* show (Dijon, 1994) a relaxation area intended for the artists in the exhibition, equipped in particular with a table football game and a full fridge... To wind up these convivial situations being developed as part of a "friendship" culture, let us mention the bar created by Heimo Zobernig for the exhibition *Unité,* and Franz West's *Passtücke.* But other artists are suddenly emerging in the relational fabric in a more aggressive way. Douglas Gordon's work, for example, explores the "wild" dimension of this interactivity, by acting parasitically and paradoxically in the social space. So he phoned the customers in a café, and sent multiple "instructions" to selected people. The best example of untimely communication upsetting communication networks is probably Angus Fairhurst's piece, for which, with the help of airwave-pirating equipment, he linked two art galleries telephonically together. Each person at the other end of the line thought it was the other person who had called, so their exchanges would end up in an improbable misunderstanding... As creations and explorations of relational schemes, these works form relational microterritories displayed in the depth of the contemporary "socius": experiences publicised by surface-objects (Liam Gillick's boards, Pierre Huyghe's posters made in the street, and Eric Duyckaerts' video-lectures), or else given over to immediate experience (Andrea Fraser's exhibition tours).

Collaborations and contracts
Those artists proposing as artworks:
a/ moments of sociability
b/ objects producing sociability,
also sometimes use a relational context defined in advance so as to
extract production principles from it. The exploration of relations
existing between, for instance, the artist and his/her gallery owner
may determine forms and a project. Dominique Gonzalez-Foerster,
whose work deals with the relations which link lived life with its
media, images, spaces and objects, has thus devoted several
exhibitions to the biographies of her gallery owners. *Bienvenue à ce
que vous croyez voir (welcome to What You Think You're Seeing)*
(1988) included photographic documentation about Gabrielle
Maubrie, and *The Daughter of a Taoist* (1992) used a set inspired by
intimism to mix Esther Schipper's childhood memories with objects
formally organised according to their evocative potential and their
colour range (here, a predominant red). Gonzalez-Foerster thus
explores the unspoken contract that binds the gallery owner to
"his/her" artist, the former being an integral part of the other's
personal history, and vice versa. It goes without saying that those
fragmented biographies, where the main factors are provided in the
form of "hints" and "clues" by the person commissioning the work,
conjure up the portrait tradition, when the commission formed the
social bond at the root of artistic representation. Maurizio Cattelan
has also worked directly on the physical person of his gallery owners:
by designing a phallic rabbit costume for Emmanuel Perrotin, which
he had to wear throughout the exhibition, and by earmarking clothes
for Stefano Basilico creating the illusion that he was carrying gallery
owner Ileana Sonnabend on his shoulders... In a more circuitous
way, Sam Samore asks gallery owners to take photographs which he
then selects and reframe. But this artist/curator pairing, which is an
intrinsic part of the institution, is just the literal aspect of inter-human
relations likely to define an artistic production. Artists take things
further, by working with spectacle figures; whence Dominique

Gonzalez-Foerster's work with the actress Maria de Medeiros (1990); the series of public activities organised by Philippe Parreno for the imitator Yves Lecoq, through which it was his intent to refashion, from within, the image of a television person (*Un homme public*, Marseille, Dijon, Ghent, 1994-1995).

Noritoshi Hirakawa, for his part, produces forms based on set up meetings. So for his show at the Pierre Huber Gallery in Geneva (1994) he published a small ad to recruit a girl who would agree to travel with him in Greece, a visit that would be the material for the show. The images he exhibits are always the outcome of a specific contract drawn up with his model, who is not necessarily visible in the photos. In other instances, Hirakawa uses a particular corporate body, as when he asked several fortune-tellers to predict his future; He records their predictions that could then be listened to with a walkman, alongside photos and slides conjuring up the world of clairvoyance. For a series titled *Wedding Piece* (1992), Alix Lambert investigated the contractual bonds of marriage: in six months, she got married to four different people, divorcing them all in record time. In this way, Lambert put herself inside the "adult role-playing" represented by the institution of marriage, which is a factory where human relations are reified. She exhibits objects produced by this contractual world-certificates, official photos and other souvenirs... The artist here becomes involved in form-producing worlds (visit to the fortune-teller, officialization of a liaison, etc.) which pre-exist him or her, material that is available for anyone to use. Some artistic events, with *Unité* still the best example (Firminy, June 1993), enabled artists to work in a formless relational model, as the one offered by the residents of a large housing complex. Several of those taking part worked directly on modifying and objectivizing social relations, one such being the Premiata Ditta group, which systematically questioned the inhabitants of the building where the exhibition was being held, so as to compile statistics. Then there is Fareed Armaly, whose installation based on sound documents included interviews with tenants, which could be listened to with headphones. Clegg & Guttman, for their part, presented in the middle of their work a kind of bookshelf unit, the shape of which suggested the architecture of Le Corbusier, and was designed to hold on tapes each inhabitant's favourite pieces of music. The cultural customs of the residents were thus objectivized by an architectonic structure, and grouped on tape, floor by floor, thus forming compilations that could be consulted by all and sundry throughout the exhibition... As a form fuelled and produced by collective interaction, Clegg & Guttman's *Record lending library*, whose principle was once more used for the *Backstage* show at the Hamburg Kunstverein in that same year, embodies in its own right this contractual system for the contemporary artwork.

Professional relation: clienteles
As we have seen, these various ways of exploring social bonds have to do with already existing types of relations, which the artist fits into, so that he/she can take forms from them. Other practices are aimed at recreating socio-professional models and applying their production methods. Here, the artist works in the real field of the production of goods and services, and aims to set up a certain ambiguity, within the space of his activity, between the utilitarian function of the objects he is presenting, and their aesthetic function. It is this wavering between contemplation and use that I have tried to identify by the term: operative realism[4], with artists as diverse as Peter Fend, Mark Dion, Dan Peterman and Niek Van de Steeg in mind, as well as more or less parody-oriented "businesses" like Ingold Airlines and Premiata Ditta. (The same term might be used for pioneers such as Panamarenko and the John Latham's "Artist's Placement Group"). What these artists have in common is the modelling of a professional activity, with the relational world issuing therefrom, as a device of artistic production. These make-believe phenomena which imitate the general economy, as is the case with Ingold Airlines, Servaas Inc., and Mark Kostabi's "studio", are limited to a construction of the replicas of an airline company, a fishery and a production workshop, but without learning any

ideological and practical lessons from doing so, and thus being restricted to a parody-like dimension of art. The example of the *Les ready-mades appartiennent à tout le monde (Ready-mades Belong to Everyone)* agency, headed by the late Philippe Thomas, is a bit different. He did not have time to proceed in a credible way to a second stage, because his signature casting project ran somewhat out of steam after the *Feux Pales (Pale Fires)* (1990) exhibition at the Capc in Bordeaux. But Philippe Thomas' system, in which the pieces produced are signed by their purchaser, shed light on the cloudy relational economics that underpin the relations between artist and collector. A more discreet narcissism lies at the root of the pieces shown by Dominique Gonzalez-Foerster at the ARC in Paris and the Capc in Bordeaux[5]. These were Biographical Offices where, with no more than an appointment, the visitor came to divulge the salient facts of his life, with a view to a biography that would then be formalised by the artist.

Through little services rendered, the artists fill in the cracks in the social bond. Form thus really becomes the "face looking at me". This is Christine Hill's modest aim, when she becomes involved in the most menial of tasks (giving massages, shining shoes, working at a supermarket check-out, organising group meetings etc.), driven by the anxiety caused by the feeling of uselessness. So through little gestures art is like an angelic programme, a set of tasks carried out beside or beneath the real economic system, so as to patiently re-stitch the relational fabric. Carsten Höller, for his part, applies his high-level scientific training to the invention of situations and objects which involve human behaviour: inventing a drug that releases a feeling of love, Baroque sets, and para-scientific experiments. Others, like Henry Bond and Liam Gillick as part of the *Documents* projects embarked upon in 1990, adjust their function to a precise context. By becoming acquainted with information just as it "came through" on press agency teleprinters, Bond and Gillick would hasten to the places where the thing was happening at the same time as their "colleagues", and bring back an image that was completely out of synch when compared with the usual criteria of the profession. In any event, Bond and Gillick strictly applied the production methods of the mainstream press, just as Peter Fend, with his OECD company, and Niek Van de Steeg put themselves in the architect's working conditions. By conducting themselves inside the art world on the basis of the parameters of "worlds" that are heterogeneous to it, these artists here introduce relational worlds governed by concepts of clientele, order or commission, and project. When Fabrice Hybert exhibited at the Musée d'Art Moderne de la ville de Paris in February 1995, all the industrial products actually or metaphorically contained in his work, as directly dispatched by their manufacturers and earmarked for sale to the public through his company "UR" (Unlimited responsibility), he puts the beholder in an awkward position. This project, which is as removed from Guillaume Bijl's illusionism as from an imitative reproduction of mercantile trade, focuses on the desiring dimension of the economy. Through his import-export activity dealing with seating bound for North Africa, and the transformation of the Musée d'Art Moderne de la ville de Paris into a supermarket, Hybert defines art as a social function among others, a permanent "digestion of data", the purpose of which is to rediscover the "initial desires that presided over the manufacture of objects".

How to occupy a gallery
The exchanges that take place between people, in the gallery or museum space, turn out to be as likely to act as the raw matter for an artistic work. The opening is often an intrinsic part of the exhibition set-up, and the model of an ideal public circulation: a prototype of this being Yves Klein's *L'exposition du vide*, in April 1958. From the presence of Republican guards at the entrance to the Iris Clert Gallery to the blue cocktail offered to visitors, Klein tried to control every aspect of the routine opening protocol, by giving each one a poetic function defining its object: the void. Thus, to mention a work still having repercussions, the work of Julia Scher (*Security by Julia*) consists in placing surveillance apparatus

in exhibition venues. It is the human flow of visitors, and its possible regulation, which thus becomes the raw material and the subject of the piece. Before long, it is the entire exhibition process that is "occupied" by the artist.

In 1962, Ben lived and slept in the One Gallery in London for a fortnight, with just a few essential props. In Nice, in August 1990, Pierre Joseph, Philippe Parreno and Philippe Perrin also "lived in" the Air de Paris Gallery, literally and figuratively, with their show *Les Ateliers du Paradise.* It might be hastily concluded that this was a remake of Ben's performance, but the two projects refer to two radically different relational worlds, which are as different in terms of their ideological and aesthetic foundation as their respective period can be. When Ben lived in the gallery, it was his intent to signify that the arena of art was expanding, and even included the artist's sleep and breakfasts. On the other hand, when Joseph, Parreno and Perrin occupied the gallery, it was to turn it into a production workshop, a "photogenic space" jointly managed by the viewer, in accordance with very precise rules of play. At the opening of *Les Ateliers du Paradise*, where everyone was rigged out in a personalised T-shirt ("Fear", "Gothic", etc.), the relations that were struck up among visitors turned into a while-you-wait script, written live by the film-maker Marion Vernoux on the gallery computer. The interplay of inter-human relations was thus materialised in compliance with the principles of an interactive video game, a "real time film" experienced and produced by the three artists. A lot of outside people thus helped to build a space of relations, not only other artist but psychoanalysts, coaches, friends... This type of "real time" work, which tends to blur creation and exhibition, was taken up by the exhibition *Work, Work in Progress. Work* at the Andrea Rosen Gallery (1992), with Felix Gonzalez-Torres, Matthew McCaslin and Liz Larner, and then by *This is the show and the show is many things*, which was held in Ghent in October 1994, before finding a more theoretical form with the *Traffic* exhibition that I curated. In both instances, each artist was at leisure to do what he/she wanted throughout the exhibition, to alter the piece, replace it, or propose performances and events. With each modification, as the general setting evolved, the exhibition played the part of a flexible matter, "informed" by the work of the artist. The visitor here had a crucial place, because his interaction with the works helped to define the exhibition's structure. He was faced with devices requiring him to make a decision. In Gonzalez-Torres' *Stacks* and piles of sweets, for example, the visitor was authorised to take away something from the piece (a sweet, a sheet of paper), but it would purely and simply disappear if every visitor exercised this right: the artist thus appealed to the visitor's sense of responsibility, and the visitor had to understand that his gesture was contributing to the break-up of the work. What position should be adopted when looking at a work that hands out its component parts while trying to hang on to its structure? The same ambiguity awaited the viewer of his *Go-go Dancer* (1991), a young man wearing a g-string on a minimal plinth, or the person looking at *personnages vivants à réactiver*, which Pierre Joseph accommodates in the exhibitions at the opening. Looking at *The female beggar* brandishing her rattle (*No man's time*, Villa Arson, Nice, 1991), it is impossible not to avert the eye, enmeshed in its aesthetic designs, which reifies, no precautions taken, a human being by assimilating it to the artworks surrounding it. Vanessa Beecroft juggles with a similar chord, but keeps the beholder at a distance. At her first one-woman show, with Esther Schipper in Cologne, November 1994, the artist took photos, among a dozen girls all wearing identical thin polo-neck jumpers and panties, and all in blonde wigs, while a barrier preventing entrance to the gallery enabled two or three visitors at a time to check out the scene, from a distance. Strange groups of people, under the curious gaze of a voyeur viewer: Pierre Joseph characters coming from a fantastic popular imaginary, two twin sisters exhibited beneath two pictures by Damien Hirst (Art Cologne, 1992), a stripper performing her show (Dike Blair), a walker walking on a moving walkway, in a truck with see-through sides following the random itinerary of a Parisian

(Pierre Huyghe, 1993), a stallholder playing a barrel-organ with a monkey on a lead (Meyer Vaisman, Jablonka Gallery, 1990), rats fed on "Bel Paese" cheese by Maurizio Cattelan, poultry rendered inebriated by Carsten Höller with the help of bits of bread soaked in whisky (collective video, *Unplugged,* 1993), butterflies attracted by glue-steeped monochrome canvases (Damien Hirst, *In and out of Love*, 1992), animals and human beings bumping into each other in galleries acting as test-tubes for experiments to do with individual and social behaviour. When Joseph Beuys spent a few days locked with a coyote (*I like America and America likes me*), he gave himself over to a demonstration of his powers, pointing to a possible reconciliation between man and the "wild" world. On the other hand, as far as most of the above-mentioned pieces are concerned, their author has no preordained idea about what would happen: art is made in the gallery, the same way that Tristan Tzara thought that "thought is made in the mouth".

1. Pierre Bourdieu, *Raisons pratiques*, Editions du Seuil, p. 68.
2. *Cf.* writings of Lucy Lippard such as *Dematerialization of the artwork*, and Rosalind Krauss, *Sculpture in the Expanded Field*, etc.
3. Félix Guattari, *Molecular Revolution*, Penguin, 1984.
4. On this concept, we should mention two writings: "*Qu'est-ce que le réalisme opératif*", in the catalogue for *Il faut construire l'Hacienda*, CCC Tours, January 1992. "Produire des rapports au monde", in the catalogue for *Aperto*, Venice Biennial, 1993.
5. Exhibition *L'Hiver de l'amour*, and *Traffic*.

Space-time exchange factors

Artworks and exchanges

Because art is made of the same material as the social exchanges, it has a special place in the collective production process. A work of art has a quality that sets it apart from other things produced by human activities. This quality is its (relative) social transparency. If a work of art is successful, it will invariably set its sights beyond its mere presence in space: it will be open to dialogue, discussion, and that form of inter-human negotiation that Marcel Duchamp called "the coefficient of art", which is a temporal process, being played out here and now. This negotiation is undertaken in a spirit of "transparency" which hallmarks it as a product of human labour. The work of art actually shows (or suggests) not only its manufacturing and production process, its position within the set of exchanges, and the place, or function, it allocates to the beholder, but also the creative behaviour of the artist (otherwise put, the sequence of postures and gestures which make up his/her work, and which each individual work passes on like a sample or marker). So every canvas produced by Jackson Pollock so closely links the flow of paint to an artist's behaviour, that the latter seems to be the image of the former, like its "necessary product", as Hubert Damisch[1] has written. At the beginning of art we find the behaviour adopted by the artist, that set of moods and acts whereby the work acquires its relevance in the present. The "transparency" of the artwork comes about from the fact that the gestures forming and informing it are freely chosen or invented, and are part of its subject. For example, over and above the popular icon represented by the image of Marilyn Monroe, the sense of Andy Warhol's *Marilyn* stems from the industrial production process adopted by the artist, governed by an altogether mechanical indifference to the subjects selected by him. This "transparency" of artistic work contrasts, need it be said, with the sacred, and with those ideologies which seek in art the means of giving the religious a new look. This relative transparency, which is an a priori form of artistic exchange, seems intolerable to the bigot. We know that, once introduced into the exchange circuit, any kind of production takes on a social form which no longer has anything to do with its original usefulness. It acquires an *exchange value* that partly covers and shrouds its primary "nature". The fact is that a work of art has no a priori useful function-not that it is socially useless, but because it is available and flexible, and has an "infinite tendency". In other words, it is devoted, right away, to the world of exchange and communication, the world of "commerce", in both meanings of the term. What all goods have in common is the fact that they have a value, that is, a common substance that permits their exchange. This substance, according to Marx, is the "*amount of abstract labour*" used to produce this item. It is represented by a sum of money, which is the "*abstract general equivalent*" of all goods between them. It has been said of art, and Marx was the first, that it represents the "*absolute merchandise*", because it is the actual image of the value.

But what exactly are we talking about? About the art object, not about artistic practice, about the work as it is assumed by the general economy, and not its own economy. Art represents a barter activity that cannot be regulated by any currency, or any "common substance". It is the division of meaning in the wild state-an exchange whose form is defined by that of the object itself, before being so defined by definitions foreign to it. The artist's practice, and his behaviour as producer, determines the relationship that will be struck up with his work. In other words, what he produces, first and foremost, is relations between people and the world, by way of aesthetic objects.

The subject of the artwork
Every artist whose work stems from relational aesthetics has a
world of forms, a set of problems and a trajectory which are all his
own. They are not connected together by any style, theme or
iconography. What they do share together is much more decisive,
to wit, the fact of operating within one and the same practical and
theoretical horizon: the sphere of inter-human relations. Their
works involve methods of social exchanges, interactivity with the
viewer within the aesthetic experience being offered to him/her,
and the various communication processes, in their tangible
dimension as tools serving to link individuals and human groups
together.
So they are all working within what we might call the relational
sphere, which is to today's art what mass production was to Pop Art
and Minimal Art.
They all root their artistic praxis within a *proximity* which
relativizes the place of visuality in the exhibition protocol, without
belittling it. The artwork of the 1990s turns the beholder into a
neighbour, a direct interlocutor. It is precisely the attitude of this
generation toward communications that makes it possible to define
it in relation to previous generations. Most artists emerging in the
1980s, from Richard Prince to Jeff Koons by way of Jenny Holzer,
developed the visual aspect of the media, while their successors
show a preference for contact and tactility. They prefer *immediacy*
in their visual writing. This phenomenon has a sociological
explanation, given that the decade that has just gone by, marked as
it was by the recession, turned out to be not very propitious to
spectacular and showy undertakings. There are also purely
aesthetic reasons for this: the "back to" pendulum came to a halt in
the 1980s on movements from the 1960s, and mainly Pop Art,
whose visual effectiveness underpins most of the forms proposed
by *simulationism*. For better or for worse, our era is identified, right
down to its crisis "ambience ", with the "poor" and experimental art
of the 1970s. This albeit superficial voguish effect made it possible

to re-view the works of artists like Gordon Matta-Clark and Robert Smithson, while the success of Mike Kelley recently encouraged a rereading of Californian "Junk Art", from Paul Thek to Tetsumi Kudo. Fashion also creates aesthetic microclimates, the effects of which have repercussions even on our reading of recent history. Otherwise put, the sieve organises the mesh of its net in different ways, and "lets through" other types of works-which, in return, influence the present.

This said, we find ourselves, with relational artists, in the presence of a group of people who, for the first time since the appearance of Conceptual Art in the mid sixties, in no way draw sustenance from any re-interpretation of this or that past aesthetic movement. Relational art is not the revival of any movement, nor is it the comeback of any style. It arises from an observation of the present and from a line of thinking about the fate of artistic activity. Its basic claim-the sphere of human relations as artwork venue-has no prior example in art history, even if it appears, after the fact, as the obvious backdrop of all aesthetic praxis, and as a modernist theme to cap all modernist themes. Suffice it merely to re-read the lecture given by Marcel Duchamp in 1954, titled "The Creative Process", to become quite sure that interactivity is anything but a new idea...
Novelty is elsewhere. It resides in the fact that this generation of artists considers inter-subjectivity and interaction neither as fashionable theoretical gadgets, not as additives (alibis) of a traditional artistic practice. It takes them as a point of departure and as an outcome, in brief, as the main informers of their activity. The space where their works are displayed is altogether the space of interaction, the space of openness that ushers in all dialogue (Georges Bataille would have written: "rift" ("*déchirure*")). What they produce are relational space-time elements, inter-human experiences trying to rid themselves of the straitjacket of the ideology of mass communications, in a way, of the places where alternative forms of sociability, critical models and moments of constructed conviviality are worked out. It is nevertheless quite

clear that the age of the New Man, future-oriented manifestos, and calls for a better world all ready to be walked into and lived in is well and truly over. These days, utopia is being lived on a subjective, everyday basis, in the real time of concrete and intentionally fragmentary experiments. The artwork is presented as a *social interstice* within which these experiments and these new "life possibilities" appear to be possible. It seems more pressing to invent possible relations with our neighbours in the present than to bet on happier tomorrows. That is all, but it is quite something. And in any event it represents a much-awaited alternative to the depressive, authoritarian and reactionary thinking which, in France at least, passes for art theory in the form of "common sense" rediscovered. Modernity, however, is not dead, if we acknowledge as modern a soft spot for aesthetic experience and adventurous thinking, as contrasted with the cautious forms of conventionality being defended by our freelance philosophers, the neo-traditionalists ("Beauty" according to the priceless Dave Hickey) and those backward-looking militant such as Jean Clair. Whatever these fundamentalists clinging to yesterday's *good taste* may say and think, present-day art is roundly taking on and taking up the legacy of the 20th century avant-gardes, while at the same time challenging their dogmatism and their teleological doctrines. Rest assured that much pondering went into this last sentence: it is simply time to write it down. For modernism was steeped in an "imaginary of contrasts", to borrow Gilbert Durand's term, which proceeded by way of separations and contrasts, readily disqualifying the past in favour of the future. It was based on conflict, whereas the imaginary of our day and age is concerned with negotiations, bonds and co-existences. These days we are no longer trying to advance by means of conflictual clashes, by way of the invention of new assemblages, possible relations between distinct units, and alliances struck up between different partners. Aesthetic contracts, like social contracts, are abided by for what they are. Nobody nowadays has ideas about ushering in the golden age on Earth, and we are readily prepared just to create various forms of *modus vivendi* permitting fairer social relations, more compact ways of living, and many different combinations of fertile existence. Art, likewise, is no longer seeking to represent utopias; rather, it is attempting to construct concrete spaces.

Space-time factors in 1990s' art
These "relational" procedures (invitations, casting sessions, meetings, convivial and user-friendly areas, appointments, etc.) are merely a repertory of common forms, vehicles through which particular lines of thought and personal relationships with the world are developed. The subsequent form that each artist gives to this relational production is not unalterable, either. These artists perceive their work from a threefold viewpoint, at once aesthetic (how is it to be "translated" in material terms?), historical (how is to be incorporated in a set of artistic references?) and social (how is to find a coherent position with regard to the current state of production and social relations?). These activities evidently acquire their formal and theoretical marks in Conceptual Art, in Fluxus and in Minimal Art, but they simply use these like a vocabulary, a lexical basis. Jasper Johns, Robert Rauschenberg and the New Realists all relied on the readymade to develop both their rhetoric about the object, and their sociological discourse. When relational art makes reference to conceptual and Fluxus-inspired situations and methods, or to Gordon Matta-Clark, Robert Smithson and Dan Graham, it is to convey lines of thought which have nothing to do with their own thinking. The real question is more likely this: what are the *right* exhibition methods in relation to the cultural context and in relation to the history of art as it is being currently updated? Video, for example, is nowadays becoming a predominant medium. But if Peter Land, Gillian Wearing and Henry Bond, to name just three artists, have a preference for video recording, they are still not "video artists". This medium merely turns out to be the one best suited to the formalisation of certain activities and projects. Other

artists thus produce a systematic documentation about their work, thereby drawing the lessons of Conceptual Art, but on radically different aesthetic bases. Relational art, which is well removed from the administrative rationality that underpins it (the form of the notarised contract, ubiquitous in the sixties' art), tends to draw inspiration more from the flexible processes governing ordinary life. We can use the term communications, but here, too, today's artists are placed at the other extreme, compared with how artists made use of the media in the previous decade. Where these artists tackled the visual form of mass communications and the icons of pop culture, Liam Gillick, Miltos Manetas and Jorge Pardo work on scaled-down models of communicational situations. This can be interpreted as a change in the collective sensibility. Henceforth the group is pitted against the mass, neighbourliness against propaganda, low tech against high tech, and the tactile against the visual. And above all, the everyday now turns out to be a much more fertile terrain than "pop culture" –a form that only exists in contrast to "high culture", through it and for it.

To head off any polemic about a so-called return to "conceptual" art, let us bear in mind that these works in no way celebrate immateriality. None of these artists has a preference for "performances" or concept, words that no longer mean a whole lot here. In a word, the work process no longer has any supremacy over ways of rendering this work material (unlike Process Art and Conceptual Art, which, for their part, tended to fetishize the mental process to the detriment of the object). In the worlds constructed by these artists, on the contrary, objects are an intrinsic part of the language, with both regarded as vehicles of relations to the other. In a way, an object is every bit as immaterial as a phone call. And a work that consists in a dinner around a soup is every bit as *material* as a statue. This arbitrary division between the gesture and the forms it produces is here called into question, insofar as it is the very image of contemporary alienation: the cannily maintained illusion, even in art institutions, that objects excuse methods and that the *end* of art justifies the pettiness of the intellectual and ethical means. Objects and institutions, and the use of time and works, are at once the outcome of human relations-for they render social work concrete-and producers of relations-for, conversely, they organise types of sociability and regulate inter-human encounters. Today's art thus prompts us to envisage the relations between space and time in a different way. Essentially, moreover, it derives its main originality from the way this issue is handled. What, actually, is *concretely produced* by artists such as Liam Gillick, Dominique Gonzalez-Foerster and Vanessa Beecroft? What, in the final analysis, is the object of their work? To introduce a few comparative factors, we should have to embark upon a history of the use value of art. When a collector purchased a work by Jackson Pollock or Yves Klein, he was buying, over and above its aesthetic interest, a milestone in a history on the move. He became the purchaser of a historical situation. Yesterday, when you bought a Jeff Koons, what was being brought to the fore was the hyper-reality of artistic value. What has one bought when one owns a work by Tiravanija or Douglas Gordon, other than a relationship with the world rendered concrete by an object, which, *per se*, defines the relations one has towards this relationship: the relationship to a relationship?

1. Hubert Damisch, *Fenêtre jaune cadmium*, Editions du Seuil, p. 76.

Joint presence and availability:
The theoretical legacy of Felix Gonzalez-Torres

The work involved here is a smallish cube of paper, not big enough to give an impression of monumentality, and too stark to enable you to forget that it was just a stack of identical posters. It is sky-blue in colour, with broad white piping acting as a frame. On the edge the blue was heightened by the pile of paper. The notice read: Felix Gonzalez-Torres, *Untitled (Blue Mirror)*, 1990. *Offset print on paper, endless copies.* One is allowed to take one of the posters away with him/her. But what happens if lots of visitors walk off in turn with these sheets of paper offered to an abstract public? What process would cause the piece to change and then vanish? For this work did not involve a "Performance", or a poster hand-out, but a work endowed with a defined form and a certain density, a work not displaying its construction (or dismantlement) process, but *the form of its presence* amid an audience. This set of issues to do with the convivial offering and the availability of the work of art, as produced and staged by Gonzalez-Torres, turn out, today, to be meaningful. Not only are they at the hub of contemporary aesthetics, but they go a whole lot further too, extending to our relations with things. This is why, after his death in 1996, the Cuban artist's work calls for a critical appraisal in order to reinstate it in the present-day context, to which it has made a conspicuous contribution.

Homosexuality as a paradigm of cohabitation

It would be too easy to comply with a currently widespread trend and reduce Felix Gonzalez-Torres' work to a neo-formalist set of problems or an agenda for gay activism. Its strength lies at once in the artist's skilful instrumentalization of forms, and in his ability to side-step community-oriented identifications to get to the heart of the human experience. So, for him, homosexuality represented not so much a discursive theme than an emotional dimension, a form of life creating forms of art. Felix Gonzalez-Torres was probably the very first person to convincingly posit the bases of a homo-sensual aesthetics, in the sense that inspired Michel Foucault to advance a creative ethics of love relationships. What is involved, in both instances, is an enthusiasm for the universal, and not a categorising claim. With Gonzalez-Torres, homosexuality did not seal a community assertion: quite to the contrary, it became a life model that could be shared by all, and identified with by everyone.

Furthermore, it gave rise in his work to a specific realm of forms, hallmarked mainly by a contrastless duality. The figure "two" is ubiquitous, but it is never a binary contrast. We thus see two clocks with their hands stopped at the same time (*Untitled (Perfect Lovers)*, 1991); two pillows on a crumpled bed, still bearing the signs of a body (24 posters, 1991); two bare light bulbs fixed to the wall, with intertwined wires (*Untitled (March 5th) # 2*, 1991); two mirrors set side by side (*Untitled (March 5th) #1*, 1991); the basic unit of Gonzalez-Torres' aesthetic is twofold, and dual. The feeling of loneliness is never represented by the "1", but the absence of the "2". This is why his work was a significant moment in the representation of the couple, a classic figure in the history of art. This is no longer the addition of two inevitably heterogeneous realities, complementing one another in a subtle interplay of contrasts and dissimilarities, and driven by the ambivalence of the motions of attraction and repulsion (suffice it to think of Van Eyck's *The Marriage of Giovanni*

Arnolfini and Giovanna Cenami, or the Duchampian "king and queen" symbolism). Gonzalez-Torres' couple, on the other hand, is typified as a tranquil, twofold unit, or an ellipse (*Untitled (Double Portrait)*, 1991). The formal structure of his work lies in this harmonious parity, and in this inclusion of the other in the self, which is endlessly declined and which certainly represents its main paradigm. It is tempting to describe his work as autobiographical, given the many allusions the artist made to his own life (the highly personal tone of the *puzzles*, the appearance of the *candy pieces* just when his boyfriend Ross died), but this idea has something incomplete about it. From start to finish, Gonzalez-Torres told the tale not of an individual, but of a couple, thus cohabitation. The work is also divided into figures which all have a close relationship with lovers living together. Meeting and coming together (all the "pairs"); knowledge of the other (the "portraits"); life shared, presented like a string of happy moments (the light bulbs and the travel figures); separation, including all the imagery of absence which is ubiquitous in the work; illness (the record of *Untitled (Bloodworks)*, 1989; the red and white beads of *Untitled (Blood)*, 1992); and last of all the lament of death (Stein and Toklas' grave in Paris; the black edging on the white posters).

Overall, Gonzalez-Torres' work is well and truly organised around an autobiographical project, but a two headed, shared autobiography. So from the mid eighties onward, when the Cuban artist had his first shows, he foreshadowed a space based in inter-subjectivity, which is precisely the space that would be explored by the most interesting artists of the next decade. To mention just a few, whose work is now coming to maturity, Rirkrit Tiravanija, Dominique Gonzalez-Foerster, Douglas Gordon, Jorge Pardo, Liam Gillick and Philippe Parreno, who each develop their personal problem-set, but also find common ground around the priority they give to the space of human relations in the conception and distribution of their works (they express ways of production based on inter-human relations). Dominique Gonzalez-Foerster and Jorge Pardo are perhaps the two artists with the most points in common with Gonzalez-Torres: the former by dint of his exploration of household intimacy as an interface of the movements of the public imaginary, turning the most personal and complex memories into clear, spare forms; the latter as a result of the minimal, evanescent, subtle aspect of his formal repertory, and his ability to solve space-time problems by the geometrization of functional objects. Gonzalez-Foerster and Pardo alike both put colour at the centre of their concerns. The fact is that it is often possible to recognise Gonzalez-Torres' "style" by its chromatic softness (blue sky and white everywhere; red is only introduced to indicate blood, the new figure of death).

The idea of *including the other* is not just a theme. It turns out to be as essential to the formal understanding of the work. There has been a great deal of emphasis on the way Gonzalez-Torres "refills" now historicized forms, and his re-use of the aesthetic repertory of Minimal Art (the paper cubes; the diagrams resembling Sol LeWitt drawings), anti-form and process art (the candy corners call to mind Richard Serra in the late sixties) and Conceptual Art (the white on black poster-portraits are reminiscent of Kosuth). But here, too, what is at issue is pairing and co-existence. The persistent issue raised by Gonzalez-Torres might be summed up thus: "How can I live in your reality?" or: "How can a meeting between two realities alter them bilaterally?"... The injection of the artist's intimist world into the art structures of the ninety sixties created brand new situations, and retrospectively switched our reading of art towards a less formalist and more psychologically oriented line of thinking. Needless to say, this recycling also represents an aesthetic choice: it shows that artistic structures are never limited to just one set of meanings. On the other hand, the simplicity of the forms used by the artist contrasts fiercely with their tragic and militant content. But the essence is still this merging horizon aimed at by Gonzalez-Torres, this demand for harmony and cohabitation which even encompasses his relationship with art history.

Contemporary forms of the monument

The common point between all the things that we include within the umbrella terms of "work of art" lies in their ability to produce a sense of human existence (and point to possible trajectories) within this chaos called reality. And it is in the name of this definition that contemporary art sees itself being disparaged-whole sale-today, usually by those who see in the concept of "sense" or "meaning" a notion pre-existing human action. For them, a pile of paper cannot be included in the masterpiece category, as they assume the sense to be a pre-established entity, going beyond social exchanges and collective constructions. They do not want to see that the world is nothing other than a chaos that People stand up to by means of words and forms. They would like there to be ready-made sense (and its transcending moral code), an origin acting as guarantor of this sense (an order to be rediscovered) and codified rules (painting, now!). The art market turns out to be quite at one with them, with one or two exceptions. The irrational nature of the capitalist economy feels that the structural need to find a firm foothold in the certainties of faith-not for nothing does the dollar bill brandish its proud motto, "In God We Trust", and major investment in art veers usually towards values rubberstamped by common sense.

So people worry at seeing today's artists revealing processes and situations. People grumble about the "overly conceptual" aspect of their works (thus, as the sign of a sure instinct in laziness, conceding the failure to understand forms by the use of a term whose meaning is not known). But this relative immateriality of the nineties' art (which is more a sign of the priority given by these artists to time in relation to space than a desire not to produce objects) is motivated neither by an aesthetic militancy, nor by a mannerist refusal to create objects. They display and explore the process that leads to objects and meanings. The object is just a "happy ending" to the exhibition process, as Philippe Parreno explains. It does not represent the logical end of the work, but an event. A Tiravanija show, for example, does not dodge materialisation, but deconstructs the methods of making the art object into a series of events, giving it a proper time frame, which is not necessarily the conventional time frame of the picture being looked at. We must stick to our guns on this point. Present-day art has no cause to be jealous of the classical "monument" when it comes to producing long-lasting effects. Contemporary work is more than ever this "*demonstration, for everyone to come, of the possibility of creating significance by inhabiting the edge of the abyss*[1].", to borrow the words of Cornélius Castoriadis-a formal resolution which touches on eternity precisely *because it is specific and temporary.*

Felix Gonzalez-Torres seems to offer a perfect example of this ambition. He died of AIDS, after having rooted his work in an acute awareness of time spans, and of the survival of the most intangible of emotions. He paid close attention to production methods, and focused his practice on a theory of exchange and division. As an activist, he promoted new forms of artistic commitment. As a gay man, he managed to transmute his life style in terms of ethical and aesthetic values.

In a more precise way, he raised the issue of the processes of materialisation in art, and of the way our contemporaries look at new forms of materialisation. For most people, and in spite of technological development which ridicules this type of bias, the time span of an item of information and the capacity of a work of art to confront time are linked with the solidity of the materials chosen, and accordingly, and thus implicitly, with tradition. By confronting and rubbing shoulders with death as an individual,

Gonzalez-Torres bravely decided to put the problems of inscription at the core of his work.

He would even broach it from its most delicate side, in other words, based on the differing aspects of the monumental: the commemoration of events, the continuity of memory, and the materialisation of the intangible. So the appearance of the string of electric lights is connected with a secret vision that occurred in Paris in 1985: "*I looked up and immediately took a picture, because it was a happy sight*"[2]. Gonzalez-Torres earmarked the most monumental part of his work for the portraits that he produced on the basis of interviews and conversations with the people commissioning them. As friezes with an often chronological succession of private memories and historical events, the portraits produced in the manner of wall-drawings fulfil an essential function of the monument: the conjunction, within a unique form, of an individual and his times.

But this *stylisation* of social forms comes across even more clearly in the ongoing contrast which Gonzalez-Torres sets up between the importance of the events conjured up, together with their complexity and their seriousness, and the minimal nature of the forms used to conjure them up. Thus, for example, an uninformed visitor might well look at *Untitled (21 Days of Bloodwork-Steady Decline)* as a set of minimalist drawings. The fine grid and the single diagonal line crossing the space do not directly evoke the drop in white corpuscles in the blood of someone with AIDS. Once the connection has been made between these two realities (the discreetness of the drawing, and the illness), the allusive power of the work takes on a terrible scope which refers us to our constant desire not to see that, and unwittingly deny the possibility and range of the illness. Nothing is ever demonstrative or explicit in the political, monumental strategy to which the artist subscribes. In his own words, "*Two clocks side by side are more of a threat to power than the image of two guys giving each other a blow job, because it cannot use me as a rallying point in its struggle to obliterate meaning[3]."*

Gonzalez-Torres does not deliver messages: he includes facts in forms, like so many cryptic messages, or messages in bottles. Memory, here, undergoes a process of abstraction similar to those that affect human bodies: "*It 's a total abstraction; but it's the body. It's your life*", he said to his friend Ross, faced with the results of a blood test. With *Untitled (Alice B. Toklas and Gertrude Stein's Grave, Paris)*, a 1992 photograph depicting flowers planted on the shared grave of the two friends, Gonzalez-Torres ratified a fact; he posited female homosexuality as an unquestionable choice, capable of demanding respect from the most reactionary of Republican senators. Here, with the help of a simple photographic still life, he rediscovered the essence of the monumental: otherwise put, the production of a moral emotion. The fact that an artist manages to trigger this emotion, running counter to traditional procedures (a framed photo) and bourgeois moral codes (a lesbian couple), is not the least noteworthy aspect of this profoundly and intentionally *discreet* work.

The criterion of co-existence (works and individuals)
Gonzalez-Torres' art thus gives pride of place to the negotiation and construction of a cohabitation. It also contains a beholder's ethic. As such, it is part of a specific history, a history of works prompting the onlooker to become aware of the setting he finds himself in (the happenings and environments of the sixties, and in situ installations).

At a Gonzalez-Torres show, I saw visitors grabbing as many candies as their hands and pockets could hold: in doing so they were being referred to their social behaviour, their fetishism and their cumulative concept of the world... while others did not dare, or waited for the person next to them to filch a candy, before doing likewise. The candy pieces thus raise an ethical problem in an apparently anodyne form: our relationship to authority and the way museum guards use their power; our sense of moderation and the nature of our relationship to the work of art.

Insomuch as this latter represents the occasion of a physical experience based on exchange, it has to be subject to criteria similar to those which underpin our appreciation of any old constructed social reality. What nowadays forms the foundation of artistic experience is *the joint presence of beholders in front of the work*, be this work effective or symbolic. The first question we should ask ourselves when looking at a work of art is:

– Does it give me a chance to exist in front of it, or, on the contrary, does it deny me as a subject, refusing to consider the Other in its structure? Does the space-time factor suggested or described by this work, together with the laws governing it, tally with my aspirations in real life? Does it criticise what is deemed to be criticisable? Could I live in a space-time structure corresponding to it in reality?

These questions do not refer to any exaggeratedly anthropomorphic vision of art, but to a vision that is quite simply *human*. For all I know, an artist addresses his works to his contemporaries, unless he regards himself as under sentence of death, or terminally ill, or unless he espouses a fascist-fundamentalist version of History (time closed in on its sense, and origin). On the other hand, artworks which today seem to me worthy of ongoing interest are those which work like *interstices*, like space-time factors governed by an economy going beyond rules in force controlling the management of different kinds of public and audience. What strikes us in the work of this generation of artists is, first and foremost, the *democratic* concern that informs it. For art does not transcend everyday preoccupations, it confronts us with reality by way of the remarkable nature of any relationship to the world, through make-believe. Who do we want to kid into thinking that an *authoritarian art* in front of its viewers might refer to another real than that of an intolerant society, be it fantasised or accepted? At the other end of the scale, the exhibition situations presented to us by artists such as Gonzalez-Torres, and today Angela Bulloch, Carsten Höller, Gabriel Orozco and Pierre Huyghe, are governed by a concern to "give everyone their chance", through forms which do not establish any precedence, *a priori,* of the producer over the beholder (let us put it another way: no divine right authority), but rather negotiate open relationships with it, which are not resolved beforehand. This latter thus wavers between the status of passive consumer and the status of witness, associate, customer, guest, co-producer, and protagonist. So beware: we know that attitudes become forms, and we should now realise that forms prompt models of sociability.

And the forms that exhibitions take do not avoid these precautions. The spread of "curiosity cabinets", which we have been witnessing for some time, but also the elitist attitudes of certain people in art circles, attest to an absolute loathing of the public place and shared aesthetic experimentation, in favour of boudoirs earmarked for experts. The availability of things does not automatically make them commonplace. Like one of Gonzalez-Torres' piles of candies, there can be an ideal balance between form and its programmed disappearance, between visual beauty and modest gestures, between childlike wonder in front of the image and the complexity of the levels at which it is read.

The aura of artworks has shifted towards their public

Today's art, and I'm thinking of the above-mentioned artists as well as Lincoln Tobier, Ben Kinmont, and Andrea Zittel, to name just three more, encompasses in the working process the presence of the micro-community which will accommodate it. A work thus creates, within its method of production and then at the moment of its exhibition, a momentary grouping of participating viewers.

In a show at Le Magasin in Grenoble, Gonzalez-Torres altered the museum cafeteria by painting it blue, putting bunches of violets on the tables, and providing visitors with information about whales. For his one-man show at the Jennifer Flay Gallery in 1993, *Untitled (Arena)*, he installed a quadrilateral bounded by switched-on light bulbs; a pair of Walkman was provided for visitors, so that they could dance under the fairy lights, noiselessly in the middle of the gallery. In both instances the artist encouraged the "beholder" to take up a position within an arrangement, giving it life, complementing the work, and taking part in the formulation of its meaning. No outcry about facile gadgets here. This kind of work (mistakenly called "*interactive*") derives from Minimal Art, whose phenomenological backdrop speculated on the presence of the viewer as an intrinsic part of the work. It is this ocular "participation" that Michael Fried denounced, incidentally, under the umbrella title of "theatricality": "*The experience of literalist art [Minimal Art] is of an object in a situation, one which, virtually by definition, includes the beholder*[4]". In its day, Minimal Art provided the tools required for a critical analysis of our perceptual conditions, and it is abundantly clear that a work like *Untitled (Arena)* no longer originates just from ocular perception: the beholder contributes his whole body, complete with its history and behaviour, and no longer an abstract physical presence. The space of Minimal Art was constructed in the distance separating eye and work. The space defined by Gonzalez-Torres' works, with the help of comparable formal wherewithal, is worked out in inter-subjectivity, in the emotional, behavioural and historical response given by the beholder to the experience proposed. The encounter with the work gives rise not so much to a space (as in the case of Minimal Art) as to a time span. Time of manipulation, understanding, decision-making, going beyond the act of "rounding off" the work by looking at it.

Modern art widely accompanied, discussed and precipitated the phenomenon of the disappearance of the aura of the work of art, as brilliantly described by Walter Benjamin in 1935. The age of "unlimited mechanical reproduction" effectively gave this para-religious effect a hard time, an effect defined by Benjamin as "the sole appearance of a distance" property conventionally associated with art. At the same time, as part of a general movement of emancipation, modernity has striven to criticise the predominance of the community over the individual, and systematically critique forms of collective alienation. So what do we find ourselves looking at today? Sacredness is making a comeback, here, there and everywhere. In a muddled way, we are hoping for the return of the traditional aura; and we don't have enough words to shout down contemporary individualism. A phase in the modern project is being wound up. Today, after two centuries of struggle for singularity and against group impulses, we must bring in a new synthesis which, alone, will be able to save us from the regressive fantasy that is abroad. Reintroducing the idea of plurality, for contemporary culture hailing from modernity, means inventing ways of being together, forms of interaction that go beyond the inevitability of the families, ghettos of technological user-friendliness, and collective institutions on offer. We can only extend modernity to advantage by going beyond the struggles it has bequeathed us. In our post-industrial societies, the most pressing thing is no longer the emancipation of individuals, but the freeing-up of inter-human communications, the dimensional emancipation of existence.

A certain suspicion creeps in with regard to mediative tools, and transitional objects in general. And thus, by extension, to the work of art regarded as a medium whereby an individual expresses his/her vision of the world in front of an audience. Relations between artists and what they produce thus tend towards the *feedback* zone. For some years now, there has been an upsurge of convivial, user-friendly artistic projects, festive, collective and participatory, exploring the varied potential in the relationship to the other. The public is being taken into account more and more. As if, henceforth, this "sole appearance of a distance" represented by the artistic aura were provided by it: as if the micro-community gathering in front of the image was becoming the actual source of the aura, the "distance" appearing specifically to create a halo around the work, which delegates its powers to it. The aura of art no longer lies in the hinter-world represented by the work, nor in form itself, but in front of it, within the temporary collective form that it produces by being put on show.

It is in this sense that we can talk of a community effect in contemporary art. It does not involve those corporate phenomena which too often act as a disguise for the most die-hard forms of conservatism (in this day and age, feminism, anti-racism and environmentalism all operate too frequently as lobbies playing the power game by enabling it never to have to call itself into question in a structural way). Contemporary art thus introduces a radical shift in relation to modern art, insomuch as it does not turn its back on the aura of the work of art, but rather moves its origin and effect. This was the thrust, some time back, of that masterpiece produced by the group General Idea, *Towards an audience vocabulary* (1977), which skipped the whole art object phase and spoke directly to the audience, offering it patterns of behaviour. The aura was recreated there, by way of free associations. But the audience concept must not be mythicized-the idea of a unified "mass" has more to do with a Fascist aesthetic than with these momentary experiences, where everyone has to hang on to his/her identity[5]. It is a matter of pre-defined cording and restricted to a contract, and not a matter of a social binding hardening around totems of identity. The aura of contemporary art is a free association.

Beauty as a solution?
Among the various reactionary temptations currently exercising
the cultural domain, we find in pride of place a project to
rehabilitate the idea of Beauty. This concept can be veiled behind
a varied terminology. We can credit Dave Hickey, the art critic
who is today's champion of this return to the norm, with calling
a spade a spade. In his essay "Invisible dragon: Four essays on
beauty[6]", Hickey is quite vague about the actual content of this
idea. The most precise definition he comes up with is this: it is a
matter of *"the agency that caused visual pleasure in the
beholder; and any theory of images that was not grounded in the
pleasure of the beholder begged the question of efficacy, and
doomed itself to inconsequence."*
There are two key notions involved here: a/ efficacy, and
b/ pleasure.
If I am to draw the necessary conclusions from this proposal, a
work of art is thus inconsequential if it is not efficacious, if it
does not show itself to be useful (in other words, by procuring a
certain degree of pleasure) to those viewing it. However I might
try to avoid disagreeable comparisons, it has to be said that this
type of aesthetic represents an example of Reagan-Thatcherite
ethics applied to art. Nowhere does Hickey challenge the nature
of this pleasure-giving "arrangement": does he regard as natural
the concepts of symmetry, harmony, sobriety and equilibrium,
which is to say, the pillars of aesthetic traditionalism, which
underlie the masterpieces of both the Renaissance and then Nazi
art?
Hickey does nevertheless make the odd point. We get a much
clearer idea of what he is referring to when he writes that "beauty
sells". Art, he goes on, must not be mistaken with idolatry and
advertising, but *"idolatry and advertising are, indeed, art, and
the greatest works of art are always and inevitably a bit of
both[7]."* As I don't get off on either of these things, I'll let the
author assume responsibility for what he writes.

To get back to the issue of beauty in art, or to what passes for such, Arthur Danto's "institutionalist" positions (and for him Art exists when institutions "recognise" a work) seem to me, alongside this torrent of fetishist irrationalism, more in compliance with the idea I have about thought. The real "nature" of the agency called *Beauty* by Hickey is extremely relative, because it is negotiation, dialogue, cultural friction and swapped viewpoints which, generation after generation, formulate the rules that govern taste. The discovery of African art, for example, profoundly altered our aesthetic canons, through a series of mediations and discussions. Let us recall that, at the end of the 19th century, all El Greco was good for was second-hand dealers, and "true" sculpture did not exist between Greek Antiquity and Donatello, But the "institutional criterion" dear to Danto seems to me to be a bit limiting, too. In this ongoing struggle to define the realm of art, many other people appear to come into the picture, from the "savage" activities of artists to reigning ideologies.

With Felix Gonzalez-Torres, however, we find an aspiration towards what Hickey calls beauty: a constant quest for simplicity and formal harmony. Let's call it an immense delicateness, that virtue that is at once visual and ethical. Never the slightest excess, or stress on effect. His work assaults neither eye nor feelings. Everything about it is implicit, discreet and fluid, unlike any cosmetic and body-built conception of "the visual impact". He is forever juggling with clichés, but these come back to life in his hands: the sight of a cloudy sky, or the photograph of a sandy beach printed on satin-finish paper, everything makes an impression although the beholder might be irked by so much kitsch. Gonzalez-Torres braces himself against subconscious emotions. So I am gripped by a childlike sense of wonder in front of the glowing, dazzling hues of piles of candies. The austerity of the "stacks" is offset by their fragile precariousness.

We might raise the objection that the artist plays here on facile emotions, that nothing is more ordinary, according to Boltanski, than these aesthetics which swiftly become emotional blackmail. But what matter is what is done with this type of emotion: what they are steered towards, how the artist organises them among themselves, and to what intent.

1. Cornélius Castoriadis, *La montée de l'insignifiance*, Editions du Seuil, 1996.

2. Guggenheim Museum catalogue,1995, p. 192.

3. *Ibid.*, p. 73.

4. Michael Fried, "Art & Objecthood" in Gregory Battock, *Minimal Art: a Critical Anthology*, Dutton, NY, p. 127.

5. On this subject, see the works of Michel Maffesoli, in particular *La Contemplation du monde*, Editions Grasset, 1993.

6. Dave Hickey, *The invisible dragon. Four essays on beauty*, Art Issues Press, Los Angeles, 1995, p. 11.

7. Dave Hickey, op. cit, p. 17.

Screen Relations

Today's art and its technological models

The modernist theory of art postulated that art and technical means were contemporary bedfellows. It believed in indissoluble bonds existing between the social order and the aesthetic order. Nowadays, we can come across in a measured and circumspect way with regard to the nature of these bonds: by noting, for example, that technology and artistic practices do not always go hand-in-hand, and that this discrepancy does no harm to either. On the one hand, the world has "broadened" under our very eyes. You would have to be unbelievably ethnocentric not to see that technological progress is far from being universal, and that the south of the planet, the so-called "developing world", does not enjoy the same reality as Silicon Valley as far as technical goods are concerned, even though both are part of an ever-narrowing world. On the other hand, our optimism with regard to the liberating power of technology has been considerably blurred. We now know that computer science, image technology and atomic energy represent threats and tools of subjugation as much as improvements to daily life. So the relationships between art and technology are much more complicated than they were in the 1960s. Let us recall that, in its day, photography did not transform the relationships between the artist and his *material*. Only the ideological conditions of pictorial practice were affected, as can be seen with impressionism. Can we create a parallel between the emergence of photography and the present-day spread of screens in contemporary exhibitions? For our age is nothing if not the age of the screen.

It is odd, moreover, that one and the same word is thus used to describe both a surface that arrests light (in the cinema) and an interface on which information is written. This collusion of meanings points to the fact that epistemological upheavals (concerning new perceptual structures), stemming from the appearance of technologies as different as film, computers, and video, are brought together around a form (the screen, the terminal) which encapsulates their various properties and potentials. By failing to conceive of this compatibility at work within our mental apparatus to attain new ways of seeing, we are doomed to a mechanistic analysis of recent art history.

Art and Goods

The Law of Relocation
Art historians are prey to two major stumbling blocks. The first is idealism, which involves seeing art as an independent realm governed exclusively by its own laws. Regarding it, in other words, to use Althusser's expression, like a train whose provenance, destination and stops are known in advance. The second and opposite one involves a mechanistic conception of history which systematically deduces from any new technological apparatus a certain number of changes in ways of thinking. It is easy to see how the relationship between art and technology is considerably less systematic. The appearance of a major invention, photography, for example, clearly alters the relationship between artists and the world, on the one hand, and methods of representation as a whole, on the other. Some things now turn out to be of no use, but others finally become possible. In the case of photography, it is the function of

realistic representation which turns out to be more and more obsolete, whereas new viewing angles become legitimised (Degas' frames) and the operational method of the camera-the rendering of the real through the impact of light-grounds the pictorial practice of the impressionist. Subsequently, modern painting would focus its issues on what it contains in terms of scaling things down to mechanical recording (matter, and gesture, which would give rise to abstract art). Then, in a third phase, artists would appropriate photography as an image-producing technique. These three attitudes which, where photography is concerned, followed on one from the other in time, may nowadays occur either simultaneously or alternately, helped by a speeding-up of exchanges. Every technical innovation that has taken place since the Second World War has thus caused a wide range of reactions among artists, from the adoption of predominant production methods (the "mec-art" of the sixties), to the preservation, come what may, of the pictorial tradition (the "purist" formalism championed by Clement Greenberg). The most fruitful thinking, however, came from artists who, far from giving up on their critical consciousness, worked on the basis of the possibilities offered by new tools, but without representing them as *techniques*. Degas and Monet thus produced a *photographic way of thinking* that went well beyond the shots of their contemporaries. We are a long way from the idea of asserting any kind of superiority of painting over the other *media*. On the other hand, we can say that art creates an awareness about production methods and human relationships produced by the technologies of its day, and that by shifting these, it makes them more visible, enabling us to see them right down to the consequences they have on day-to-day life. Technology is only of interest to artists in so far as it puts effects into perspective, rather than putting up with it as an ideological instrument.

This is what we might call the *Law of Relocation*. Art only exercises its critical duty with regard to technology from the moment when it shifts its challenges. So the main effects of the computer revolution are visible today among artists who do not use computers. On the other hand, those who produce so-called "computer graphic" images, by manipulating synthetic fractals and images, usually fall into the trap of illustration. At best, their work is just symptom or gadget, or, worse still, the representation of a symbolic alienation from the computer medium, and the representation of their own alienation from methods dictated by production. So the function of *representation* is played out in behavioural patterns. These days, it is no longer a question of depicting from without the conditions of production, but of introducing the gestural, and deciphering the social relations brought on by them. When Alighiero Boetti gets 500 weavers in Peshawar, Pakistan, working for him, he represents the work process of multinational companies much more effectively than if he merely portrayed them and described how they work. The art/technology relationship is thus particularly suited to this *operational realism* which underpins many contemporary practices, definable as the artwork wavering between its traditional function as an object of contemplation, and its more or less virtual inclusion in the socio-economic arena[1]. At least this type of practice shows up the fundamental paradox that binds art and technology together: if technology can by definition be improved, the work of art cannot. The whole difficulty encountered by artists keen to embrace the state of technology, if you'll forgive the banality of this assertion, consists in manufacturing something that will last, based on general, life-producing conditions which are essentially changeable. This is the challenge of modernity: "Taking the eternal from the transitory", yes, but also, and above all, inventing a coherent and fair *work conduct* in relation to the production methods of their time.

Technology as an ideological model
(from trace to programme)
As a producer of goods, technology expresses the state of production-oriented relationships. Photography used to tally with a given stage of development in the western economy (hallmarked by colonial expansion and the streamlining of the work process), a

stage which, in a way, called for its invention. Population control (the introduction of ID cards, and anthropometric record cards), the management of overseas wealth (ethno-photography), the need to remote-control industrial tools and find out about potential mining sites, all endowed the camera with a crucial role in the industrialisation process. In relation to this phenomenon, art's function consists in appropriating perceptual and behavioural habits brought on by the technical-industrial complex to turn them into *life possibilities*, to borrow Nietzsche's term. Otherwise put, reversing the authority of technology in order to make ways of thinking, living and seeing creative. The technology reigning over the culture of our day and age is, needless to say, computing, which we might split into two branches. On the one hand, the computer itself and the changes it has introduced and still is introducing into our way of perceiving and processing data. On the other hand, the rapid progress of user-friendly technologies, from France's "Minitel" system [originally a computerised telephone directory] to the Internet, by way of touch screens and interactive video games. The first, which affects Man's relationship with the images he produces, is making an amazing contribution to the way mentalities and attitudes are changing. With computer graphics, it is actually now possible to produce images which are the outcome of calculation, and no longer of human gestures. All the images we are acquainted with are the result of a physical action, from the hand drawing signs to wielding a camera. The existence of synthetic images, for their part, has no need of any analogous linkage to the subject. For "*the photo is the worked recording of a physical impact*", whereas "*the digital image, for its part, results not from the movement of a body, but from a calculation*[2]". The visible image no longer represents the trace of anything, unless it be that of a sequence of numbers, and its form is no longer the "terminal" of a human presence. Images "*now function on their own*" (Serge Daney), like Joe Dante's *Gremlins* which reproduced themselves by pure visual contamination. The contemporary image is typified precisely by its generative power; it is no longer a trace (retroactive), but a programme (active). Furthermore, it is this property of the digital image that informs contemporary art most powerfully. In the midst of sixties' avant-garde art, the work came across less as an independent reality than as a programme to be carried out, a model to be reproduced (for example, the games invented by Brecht and Filliou), an encouragement to be a creative oneself (Beuys) or to do something (Franz Erhard Walter). In the nineties' art, while interactive technologies developed at an exponential rate, artists were exploring the arcane mysteries of sociability and interaction. The theoretical and practical horizon of that decade's art was largely grounded in the realm of inter-human relations. So exhibitions of the work of Rirkrit Tiravanija, Philippe Parreno, Carsten Höller, Henry Bond, Douglas Gordon, and Pierre Huyghe all construct models of sociability suitable for producing human relations, the same way an architecture literally "produces" the itineraries of those residing in it. This does not however involve works about "social sculpture" the way Beuys understood it. If these artists do indeed extend the idea of *avant-garde* thrown out with the bath water of modernity (we should stress this point, even if a term with fewer connotations should be found), they are not naïve or cynical enough "to go about things as if" the radical and universalist utopia were still on the agenda. In their respect, we might talk in terms of micro-utopias, and interstices opened up in the social corpus.

These interstices work like relational programmes: world economies where there is a reversal in the relationships between work and leisure (Parreno's exhibition *Made on the 1st of May*, Cologne, May 1995), where everyone had a chance to come into contact with everybody else (Douglas Gordon), where people once again learnt what conviviality and sharing mean (Tiravanija's itinerant cafeterias), where professional relationships are treated like a festive celebration (the *Hôtel occidental* video by Henry Bond, 1993), where people are in permanent contact with the image of their work (Huyghe). The work thus proposes a functional model and not a maquette; in other words, the notion of dimension does not come into the picture, exactly as in the digital image whose proportions may vary with the size of the screen, which-unlike the frame-does not enclose works in a preordained format, but renders virtualities material in x dimensions. Projects embarked upon by today's artists have the same ambivalence as the techniques from which they are indirectly inspired. As writings in and with the real and cinematic works, they do not claim to be reality, notwithstanding. On the other hand, they make up programmes, like digital images, but without guaranteeing the applicable character of these latter, any more than the possible transcoding into formats other than the one for which they have been designed. Otherwise put, *the influence of technology on the art that is its contemporary is wielded within limits circumscribed by this latter between the real and the imaginary.*

The computer and the camera delimit production possibilities, which themselves depend on general conditions of social production, and tangible relationships existing between people. Based on this state of affairs, artists invent ways of living, or else create an awareness about a moment M in the assembly line of social behavioural patterns, making it possible to imagine a further state of our civilisation.

The camera and the exhibition

The exhibition-set
As we can see, present-day art is being developed in-depth by ways of seeing and thinking which usher in computing, on the one hand, and the video camera on the other. To get a better grasp of the degree of relationship between this paired film/programme factor and contemporary art, we must come back to the evolution of the status of the art exhibition in relation to the objects it contains. Our

hypothesis is that *the exhibition has become the basic unit* from which it is possible to conceive of relationships between art and ideology ushered in by technologies, to the detriment of the individual work. It is the cinematographic model, not as subject but as plan of action, which permitted the development of the exhibition-form in the sixties. What Marcel Broodthaers has done, for instance, is evidence of this shift from the exhibition-store (assembling noteworthy objects separately) to the exhibition-set (the unitary mise-en-scène of objects). In 1975, Broodthaers presented his green room, the latest version of the Winter Garden shown the previous year, as *"the primer for the idea of DECOR that might be typified by the idea of the object reinstated with a real function, in other words, the object here is no longer itself considered as artwork (see also pink room and blue room)*[3]." This "reinstatement" of the art object to the functional arena, a reversal which enabled Broodthaers to stand up to the "tautology of reification" which the artwork represented for him, brilliantly anticipated the artistic activities of the 1990s, and the ambiguity maintained by this between exhibition value and user value, an ambiguity exemplified by almost all the artists of that generation (from Fabrice Hybert to Mark Dion, and from Felix Gonzalez-Torres to Jason Rhoades). The exhibition *Ozone* (devised in 1988 by Dominique Gonzalez-Foerster, Bernard Joisten, Pierre Joseph and Philippe Parreno, and put on in 1989 at the APAC in Nevers and at the FRAC Corsica), which considerably opened up crucial working avenues for our period, was thus presented as a "photogenic space", that is, in accordance with a cinematographic model, the space of a virtual darkroom within which viewers evolve like a camera, called upon to frame for themselves their way of looking, and cut out viewing angles and bits of meaning. Over and above the "decor/set" according to Broodthaers, designed to dodge the inevitability of reification by the functionality of the elements making it up, *Ozone* introduced the possibility of an ongoing manipulation of its components, and the adaptation of these to the life of their possible purchaser. Devised as a "programme" giving rise to forms and situations (a "Bag" thus enabled the collector to put his own baggage together, user-friendly accessories such as seats and documents for consultation were made available to visitors), Ozone worked like an "iconographic field", a "set of information strata" (which likens it to the Broodthaers' model), while at the same time stressing values of conviviality and productivity which tipped the Belgian artist's social criticism in the direction of new horizons: among other things, the horizon of an art based on interactivity and the creation of relationships with the Other. This definition of the exhibition as a "photogenic space" was subsequently emphasised with *How We Gonna Behave* (Joisten, Joseph & Parreno, at the Max Hetzler Gallery, Cologne, 1991), where disposable cameras were placed at the Gallery entrance so that visitors could create their visual catalogues themselves.

In 1990, I tried to define these activities by talking about a "directors' art", turning the exhibition/exposition venue (by playing on the accepted meaning of this term in photography) into a filmless camera, a "still short-movie": "*The work does not (offer) itself as a spatial whole that can be scanned by the eye, but as a time span to be crossed, sequence by sequence, similar to a still short-movie in which the viewer has to evolve by himself* [4]." The fate of the cinema (or computer science), as a technology that can be used in the other arts, thus has nothing to do with the form of the film, contrary to what is maintained by the horde of opportunists who transfer on to film (or computer) lines of thinking hailing from the 19th century. So there is much more film in an Allen Ruppersberg or Cartsen Höller show than in many, perforce, blurred "artist's films", and much more computer graphic thinking in the rhizomes of the Ramo Nash Club and Douglas Gordon's activities than in those cobbled together synthetic images driven by a craftsmanship labelled as the most reactionary of the moment. How does film really inform art? By the way it handles the time factor, by the "image-movements" (Deleuze) it produces. So, as Philippe Parreno writes, art forms "*a space in which objects, images and exhibitions are split-seconds, scenarios that can be re-enacted* [5]".

Extras

The exhibition may have turned into a set, but who comes to act in it? How do the actors and extras make their way across it, and in the midst of what kind of scenery? One day, somebody ought to write the history of art using the peoples who pass through it, and the symbolic/practical structures which make it possible to accommodate them. What human *flow*, governed by what forms, thus passes into art forms? How does video, the latest variant of visual recording, alter this passage? The classic form of the on-screen presence is that of the *summons*, of the involvement of one or more actors called upon to fill a stage. So those living in Warhol's factory were one after the other press-ganged into standing in front of the camera. A film is usually based on actors, those proletarian workers who rent their image as a work force. "*The studio shot*, wrote Walter Benjamin, *is particular in that it replaces the audience by the camera*[6]", and enables the picture editing process to steal the player's body. With video, the difference between the actor and the passer-by tends to diminish. It represents the same development in relation to the film camera as that announced by the invention of paint in tubes for the impressionist generation. As light and easy-to-handle tools, they make it possible to capture things *out of doors*, and permit an offhandedness with regard to the material filmed-something that was not possible with heavy film equipment. The predominant form of videographic resident is thus *the poll*, that random foray into the crowd that typifies the television era. The camera asks questions, records movements, stays at pavement level. The ordinary humanoid inhabits video art: Henry Bond samples moments of sociability, Pierre Huyghe organises casting sessions, Miltos Manetas holds a discussion around a café table. The camera turns into an instrument for questioning people. Gillian Wearing thus asks passers-by to whistle into a Coca-Cola bottle, then edits these sequences in such a way that they produce a continuous sound-allegory of the opinion poll. In other respects, video plays the same heuristic, exploratory role as the sketch played in the 19th century. It goes along with artists, such as Sean Landers who films from his car, Angela Bulloch who records her journey from London to Genoa where she has to put up a show, and Tiravanija, again, who films his trip between Guadalajara and Madrid. Information about the work process, too, as with Cheryl Donegan who films herself producing paintings. But the manoeuvrability of video also means that it can be used as a reified replacement for presence. Hence the installation by the Italian group Premiata Ditta, placing on the table, where a conference was going on, a TV set broadcasting the picture of a man eating, oblivious to everything going an around him, conjures up those acclaimed videotapes portraying a fireplace, an aquarium, or a "disco light". The grapes of Zeuxis are still just as green for post-modern birds.

Post VCR art

Rewind/play/fast forward
The manoeuvrability of the video image is conveyed into the area where images and art forms are handled and manipulated. The basic operations we carry out with a VCR (rewind, hold, freeze frame, etc.) are now part of the array of aesthetic decisions of any artist. This applies to channel-flicking, for example. Like films, according to Serge Daney, exhibitions are becoming "disparate, zappable little programmes", where the visitor can make up his/her own itinerary. But probably the greatest change lies in the new approaches to time brought on by the presence of home video. As we have seen, the work of art is no longer presented as the mark of

a past action, but as the announcement of a forthcoming event (the "trailer effect"), or the proposal of a virtual action[7]. In any event, it is presented as a *material time span* which every exhibition event has to update and revive. The work becomes a still, a frozen moment, but one that does not do away with the flow of gestures and forms from which it stems. This latter category turns out to be by far the most numerous. To mention just a few artists who have recently emerged, Pierre Joseph's *Personnages vivants à réactiver*, together with Philippe Parreno's *Arbre d'anniversaire*, Vanessa Beecroft's living pictures (tableaux vivants) together with Fabrice Hybert's *Peintures homéopathiques*, all are presented as unified and specific time spans which can be *re-enacted*, and on which it is possible to inlay other elements and transmit a different rhythm (fast forward), just like the videos which they often end up becoming. For it would seem quite normal, today, that a piece, an action or a performance should end up becoming documentation on videotape. This forms the work's concentrated focus, which may well become watered down by heterogeneous exhibition settings. Video, as we have noted just as much in the legal domain (with the Rodney King assault, filmed by an "amateur", showing King being beaten up by the Los Angeles police) and the debate stemming from the Khaled Kelkal affair, *works like evidence*. In art, it signifies and demonstrates reality, the concreteness of a practice at times too dispersed and all over the place to be directly grasped (I'm thinking of Beecroft, Peter Land, Carsten Höller, Lothar Hempel). This artistic use of the video picture does not just happen, however. The aesthetics of conceptual art is already a factual, *witnessing* aesthetics, to do with evidence and proof; recent activities are merely following up this designation of the "completely administered world" (Adorno) in which we live, in the casual and literal mode represented by video, instead of the analytical and deconstructive mode of conceptual art.

Towards a democratisation of viewpoints?
Video apparatus is part of the democratisation of the picture-production process (as a logical follow-on from photography), but it also has an effect on our day-to-day life through the generalisation of electronic surveillance, the safety-oriented counterpoint to family video sessions. But do these latter not have something to do with surveillance? Are they not also part of a world monitored, not to say hounded, by lenses, and bogged down in procedures whereby it keeps a close eye on itself, continually recycling the forms it produces and handing them out again in different forms? *Post VCR art* renders forms nomadic and fluid, encouraging the analogous reconstruction of aesthetic objects of the past-"refills" of historicized forms. In doing so, it explains Serge Daney's prediction about film: "*The only thing that will be retained (from art) is what can be remade*[8]"... So Mike Kelley and Paul MacCarthy have had Vito Acconci's performances "re-enacted" by models, in soap opera sets (Fresh Acconci, 1995), and Pierre Huyghe filmed a scene-by-scene remake of Alfred Hitchcock's *Rear Window*, in a Paris housing estate. But if video enables (more or less) anyone to make a movie, it also makes it easier for (more or less) anyone to capture pictures of us. When we move about a city, we are under surveillance. Our very cultural works are submitted for re-reading/recycling, attesting to the ubiquity of optical instruments, and their current prevalence over any other production tool. The *Security by Julia* programme, an artistic video surveillance project "directed" by Julia Sher, explores the police, and security, related dimension of the video camera. Playing on security iconography (grills, car-park settings, monitor screens), Julia Sher turns the exhibition into a space where everyone comes both to be seen and to see their own visibility. In a group show, the Danish artist Jens Haaning set up an automatic closure mechanism which shut the visitor away in an empty room, with just a video-spy in it. Caught like an insect, the beholder was transformed into the subject of the artist's eye, represented by the camera. Over and above the obvious ethical problems posed by this kind of action (in which, in no time, relations between artist and public

become sado-masochistic), we have no option but to note that after *Present continuous past(s),* Dan Graham's extraordinary 1974 installation, which broadcast the picture of anyone venturing into it, but with a slight time lapse, the filmed visitor shifted from the status of a theatrical "character" caught in an ideology of representation to that of a pedestrian subjected to a repressive ideology of urban movement. The subject of the contemporary video is rarely free. This is because he/she collaborates in the great visual census, at once individual, sexual and ethnic, in which all forms of power agency in our society are currently indulging.

The future of art, as an instrument of emancipation, and as a political tool aimed at the liberation of forms of subjectivity, depends on the way artists deal with this issue. For art, no technique or technology is a subject. By putting technology in its productive context, by analysing its relations with the superstructure and the layer of obligatory behaviour underpinning its use, it becomes conversely possible to produce models of relations with the world, heading in the direction of modernity. Failing which, art will become an element of *high tech* deco in an increasingly disconcerting society.

1. Nicolas Bourriaud, "*Qu'est-ce que le réalisme opératif?*", in the catalogue "*Il faut construire l'hacienda*", CCC Tours; and "*Produire des rapports au monde*", in the catalogue *Aperto 93*, Venice Biennial.
2. Pierre Lévy, "*La Machine univers. Création, cognition et culture informatique*", Editions Points-Seuil, 1987, p. 50.
3. M. Broodthaers, in the catalogue "*L'angélus de Daumier*", 1975.
4. Nicolas Bourriaud, "*Un art de réalisateurs*", Art Press. no. 147, May 1990. The exhibition *Courts-métrages immobiles* was put on for the 1990 Venice Biennial.
5. Philippe Parreno, "*Une exposition serait-elle une exposition sans caméra?*", Libération, 27 May 1995.
6. W. Benjamin, *Essais II*, Editions Denoël-Gonthier, 1983, p. 105.
7. Nicolas Bourriaud, "*The Trailer Effect*" in Flash Art, 1989.
8. Serge Daney, "*Journal de l'an passé*", Trafic, no.1, Winter 1991.

Towards a policy of forms

Cohabitations
Notes on some possible extensions of a relational aesthetics

Visual systems
Eyes used to have to be raised towards the icon, which gave the divine presence a material form as an image.

In the Renaissance, the invention of centrist, monocular perspective turned the abstract beholder into a tangible, physical individual; the place allotted to him by the pictorial device likewise isolated him from others. Needless to say, everyone can look at the frescoes of Piero della Fransesca and Uccello from several viewpoints. But perspective singles out a symbolic place for the eye and gives the beholder his/her place in a symbolic social set-up.

Modern art altered this relationship by permitting many simultaneous ways of looking at pictures. But should we not be talking in terms of imports, since this manner of reading things existed already, in different forms, in Africa and the Orient?

Rothko and Pollock included in their work the need for a visual "envelope", for the picture was supposed to encompass, not to say submerge, the beholder in a chromatic ambience. We have often referred to the similarities existing between the "enveloping" effect of Abstract Expressionism and the effect sought by painters of icons. And in both cases it is an abstract humanity that is under consideration, cast whole into the pictorial space. Discussing this space enveloping the beholder in an ambience or constructed environment, Eric Troncy refers to an "all around" effect, as opposed to the "all over" style which can only be applied to flat surfaces.

The image is a moment

A representation is just a moment M of the real. All images are moments, just as any point in space is both the memory of a time x, and the reflection of a space y. Is this temporal factor frozen, or to the contrary, is it a producer of potentialities? What is an image that does not contain any forthcoming development, any "life possibility", apart from a dead image?

What artists show

So reality is what I talk about with a third party. It can only be defined as a product of negotiation. Escaping from reality is "mad". Somebody sees an orange rabbit on my shoulder, but I can't see it. So discussion weakens and shrinks. To find a negotiating space, I must *pretend* to see this orange rabbit on my shoulder. Imagination seems like a prosthesis affixed to the real so as to produce more intercourse between interlocutors. So the goal of art is to reduce the mechanical share in us. Its aim is to destroy any *a priori* agreement about what is perceived.

Similarly, meaning and sense are the outcome of an interaction between artist and beholder, and not an authoritarian fact. In modern art, I must, as beholder, make an effort to produce sense out of objects that are ever lighter, ever more impalpable and ever more volatile. Where the decorum of the picture used to offer a frame and a format, we must now often be content with bits and pieces. Feeling nothing means not making enough effort.

The boundaries of individual subjectivity

What is fascinating about Guattari is his determination to produce subjectivizing machines, and mark out every manner of situation, so as to fight against the "mass-media manufacturing" we are subject to, which is a levelling device.

The reigning ideology would have the artist be a loner, imagining him solitary and irredentist: "writing is always done alone", "we have to take refuge behind the world", blah, blah, blah... This rather naïve imagery muddles two quite different notions: the artist's refusal of the communal rules currently in force, and the refusal of the collective. If we must reject all manner of imposed communalism, it is precisely to replace it by invented relational networks.

According to Cooper, madness is not "inside" a person, but in the system of relationships of which that person is involved. People don't become "mad" all on their own, because we never think all on our own, except for postulating that the world has a centre (Bataille). No one writes or paints alone. But we have to make the pretence of so doing.

The engineering of intersubjectivity
The nineties saw the emergence of collective forms of intelligence and the "network" mode in the handling of artistic work. The popularisation of the Internet web, as well as the collectivist practices going on in the techno music scene, and more generally the increasing collectivisation of cultural leisure, have all produced a relational approach to the exhibition. Artists look for interlocutors. Because the public is always a somewhat unreal entity, artists will include this interlocutor in the production process itself. The sense of the work issues from the movement that links up the signs transmitted by the artist, as well as from the collaboration between people in the exhibition space. (After all, reality is nothing other than the passing result of what we do together, as Marx put it).

An art with no effects?
These relational artistic practices have been repeatedly criticised. Because they are restricted to the space of galleries and art centres,

they contradict the desire for sociability underpinning their meaning. They are also reproached for denying social conflict and dispute, differences and divergences, and the impossibility of communicating within an alienated social space, in favour of an illusory and elitist modelling of forms of sociability, by being limited to the art world. But do we deny the interest of Pop Art because it reproduces codes of visual alienation? Do we criticise Conceptual Art for perpetrating an angelic view of meaning? Things are not this straightforward. The principal argument held against relational art is that it supposedly represents a watered down form of social critique.

What these critics overlook is that the content of these artistic proposals has to be judged in a formal way: in relation to art history, and bearing in mind the political value of forms (what I call the "criterion of co-existence", to wit, the transposition into experience of spaces constructed and represented by the artist, the projection of the symbolic into the real). It would be absurd to judge the social and political content of a relational "work" by purely and simply shedding its aesthetic value, which would be to the liking of those who see in a Tiravanija or Carsten Höller show nothing more than a phonily utopian pantomime, as was not so very long ago being advocated by the champions of a "committed" art, in other words, propagandist art.

For these approaches do not stem from a "social" or "sociological" form of art. They are aimed at the formal space-time constructs that do not *represent* alienation, which do not *extend* the division of labour into forms. The exhibition is an interstice, defined in relation to the alienation reigning everywhere else. At times it reproduces and shifts the forms of this alienation-as in the Philippe Parreno show *Made on the lst of May* (1995), the hub of which was a leisure activity assembly line. So the exhibition does not deny the social relationships in effect, but it does distort them and project them into a space-time frame encoded by the art system, and by the artist him/herself. In a Tiravanija exhibition, for example, it is possible to see a form of naïve animation, and lament the slightness and artificiality of the moment of conviviality on offer. To my eye, this would be mistaking the object of the practice. For the purpose is not conviviality, but the *product of* this conviviality, otherwise put, a complex form that combines a formal structure, objects made available to visitors, and the fleeting image issuing from collective behaviour. In a way, the user value of conviviality intermingles with its exhibition value, within a visual project. It is not a matter of representing angelic worlds, but of producing the conditions thereof.

The political development of forms
Our day and age is certainly not short of political projects, but it is awaiting forms capable of embodying it, and thus of enabling it to become material. For form produces and shapes sense, steers it, and passes it on into day-to-day life. The revolutionary culture has created and popularised several types of sociability. The assembly (soviets, agoras), the sit-in, the demonstration and its processions, the strike and its various devices (banners, tracts, spatial organisation etc.).

Ours explores the realm of *stasis*: crippling strikes, like the one in December 1995, where time is differently organised. Free parties lasting several days, thus extending the concept of sleep and wakefulness; exhibitions on view for a whole day, and packed away after the opening; computer bugs seizing up thousands of software systems simultaneously…

Our age acquires its political effectiveness in the freezing of machinery, and the freeze-frame.

The enemy we have to fight first and foremost is embodied in a social form: it is the spread of the supplier/client relations to every level of human life, from work to dwelling-place by way of all the tacit contracts which define our private life.

French society is all the more affected because it suffers from a twofold block: national institutions are short on democracy, and the global economy is trying to force on it methods of reification which trickle into every aspect of life.

The relative failure of May' 68 in France can be seen in the low level of institutionalisation where freedoms are concerned.

The widespread failure of modernity can be found here through the way inter-human relations are turned into products, along with the impoverishment of political alternatives, and the devaluation of work as a non-economic value, to which no development of free time corresponds.

Ideology exalts the solitude of the creative person and mocks all forms of community.

Its effectiveness consists in promoting the isolation of authors by cloaking them in a smart-product extolling their "originality", but ideology is invisible: its form is being form-free. Phoney multiplicity is its greatest trick: the range of possibilities is abridged every day, while the names describing this impoverished reality proliferate.

Rehabilitating experimentation

Who are we trying to kid that it might be helpful and beneficial to stage a return to aesthetic values based on tradition, mastery of technology, and respect for historical conventions? If there is an area where chance does not exist, it is indeed the realm of artistic creation*: when we want to kill off democracy, we start by muzzling experiments, and we end up by accusing freedom of having rabies.

Relational aesthetics and constructed situations

The Situationist "constructed situation" concept is intended to replace artistic representation by the experimental realisation of artistic energy in everyday settings. If Guy Debord's diagnosis about the process of producing spectacles may strike us as harsh, the Situationist theory overlooks the fact that if the spectacle deals first and foremost with forms of human relations (it is "*a social relationship between people, with imagery as the go-between*"), it can only be analysed and fought through the production of new types of relationships between people.

The fact is that the idea of situation does not necessarily imply a co-existence with my fellow men. It is possible to imagine "constructed situations" for private use, and even intentionally barring others. The idea of "situation" extends the unity of time, place and action, in a theatre that does not necessarily involve a relationship with the Other. Artistic practice is always a relationship with the other, at the same time as it represents a relationship with the world. The *constructed situation* does not necessarily correspond to a *relational world*, formulated on the basis of a figure of exchange. Is it by coincidence that Debord divides the time of the spectacle into two, between the "exchangeable time" of work ("*endless accumulation of equivalent intervals*") and the "consumable time" of holidays, which imitates natural cycles while at the same time being a spectacle "*to a more intense degree*"? The idea of "exchangeable time" turns out, here, to be purely negative: the negative element is not the exchange per se, which is a factor of life and sociability. What Debord identifies, possibly wrongly, with the inter-human exchange are *the capitalist forms of exchange*. These forms of exchange stem from the "meeting" between the accumulation of capital (the employer) and the available work force (the employee-worker), in the form of a contract. They do not represent exchange in absolute terms, but an historical form of production (capitalism). Work time is thus less an "exchangeable time" in the fullest sense, than a *buyable* time in the form of a salary or wage-packet. The work that forms a "relational world", and a social interstice, updates Situationism and reconciles it, as far as it is possible, with the art world.

The aesthetic paradigm
(Félix Guattari and art)

Félix Guattari's work, cut short by his untimely passing, does not form a set of clear-cut pieces, with a sub-set dealing specifically with the issue of aesthetics. Art, for him, was a form of living matter rather than a category of thought, and this difference informs the very spirit of his philosophical undertaking. Over and above genres and categories, he wrote: "*The important thing is to know whether a work makes an effective contribution to a changing production of statement (production d'énonciation)*", and not to delimit the specific boundaries of this or that type of utterance. The *psyche* on the one hand, and the *socius* on the other are constructed on productive agencies, with art being just one of these, even if it enjoys a special place. Guattari's concepts are ambivalent and supple, so much so that they can be translated into many different systems. What is thus involved is the definition of a *potential* aesthetics, which only assumes a real consistency provided that it can be given a permanent transcoding. For while the practitioner in La Borde's psychiatric clinic has always granted a predominant place to the "aesthetic paradigm" in the development of his thinking, he has written very little about art, properly so-called, apart from the paper for a lecture on Balthus, and one or two passages in his major works, incorporated within a more general subject matter.

This aesthetic paradigm is nevertheless being practised already in writing itself. The style, if we may use this word, or let us rather say the Guattari scriptorial flow, encompasses every concept in a raft of images. The processes of thought are usually described here as physical phenomena, endowed with a specific texture-drifting "plates" and dovetailed "planes", "machinery", and so on. Serene materialism, where, to be effective, concepts must assume the finery of tangible reality, and become territorialized on images. Guattari's writing is informed by an obvious visual and plastic, not to say sculptural concern, yet appears to be little bothered by syntactical clarity. At times, Guattari's language may seem obscure. This is because he does not shrink from coming up with neologisms ("nationalitarian", "ritournellize") and portmanteau words, or using English and German terms as they spring to mind and flow from his pen. Nor does he shrink from embarking on propositions with regard for the reader, or juggling with the lesser meanings of an ordinary word. His phrasing is thoroughly oral, chaotic, "wild and outrageous" (délirant), off-the-cuff and littered with deceptive short-cuts, quite unlike the conceptual order that presides over the writings of accomplice and fellow Gilles Deleuze.

Guattari may still seem significantly under-estimated to us, and he is often reduced to the role of Deleuze's foil, yet it does today seem easier to acknowledge his specific contribution to the co-authored writings, from *Anti Oedipus* (1972) to *What is Philosophy?* (1991)... From the "ritournelle" concept to the masterful passages dealing with types of subjectivization, the Guattari signature stands out quite clearly, ringing out ever louder in the contemporary philosophical debate. Through its extreme particularness, and the attention it pays to the "production of subjectivity" and its preferred vehicles, the works, Félix Guattari's thinking links up right away with the productive machinery with which present-day art is riddled. In the current dearth of aesthetic thought, it thus seems to us to be increasingly useful, whatever the degree of arbitrariness affecting this operation may be, to proceed to a kind of *grafting* of Guattari's thinking in the domain of present-day art, thus creating a "polyphonic interlacing", rich in possibilities. It is a question, henceforth, of thinking about art with Guattari, and with the *toolbox* he has bequeathed us.

Subjectivity pursued and produced

De-naturalising subjectivity
The idea of subjectivity is certainly the main thread of Guattari's research. He would devote his life to dismantling the tortuous mechanisms and systems of subjectivity and putting them back together again, exploring its constituents and escape modes, and even going so far as to make it the keystone of the social edifice. Psychoanalysis and art? Two sorts of subjectivity production, inter-connected, two operational systems, two preferred tool systems, which are joined together in the possible solution to the "Malaise of Civilisation"... The pivotal position given by Guattari to subjectivity defines his conception of art, and art's value, from start to finish. In the Guattari order of things, subjectivity as *production* plays the role of a fulcrum around which forms of knowledge and action can freely pitch in, and soar off in pursuit of the laws of the socius. Which, incidentally, is what defines the field of vocabulary used to describe artistic activity. In it there is no hint of the fetishization that is common in this level of discourse. Art, here, is defined as *a process of non-verbal semiotization*, not as a separate category of global production. Uprooting fetishism to assert art as a line of thought and an "invention of life possibilities" (Nietzsche): the end purpose of subjectivity is nothing other than an individuation still to be won. Artistic practice forms a special terrain for this individuation, providing potential models for human existence in general. This is where we can define Guattari's thinking as a colossal undertaking involving the *de-naturalisation* of subjectivity, its deployment in the area of production, and the theorisation of its inclusion in the framework of the general economy of trade. There is nothing less natural than subjectivity. There is also nothing more constructed, formulated and worked on. *New forms of subjectivization are created the same way that a visual artist creates now forms from the palette at his disposal*[1]. What matters is our capacity to create new arrangements and

agencies within the system of *collective facilities* formed by the ideologies and categories of thought, a creation that shows many similarities with artistic activity. Guattari's contribution to aesthetics would be incomprehensible if we did not underline his effort to de-naturalize and deterritorialize subjectivity, expel it from his earmarked domain, the sacrosanct subject, and tackle the disconcerting shores with their proliferation of mechanistic devices and existential territories in the process of being formed. They are disconcerting because the non-human is an intrinsic part of them, contrary to the phenomenological plans with which humanist thinking is riddled. Proliferation, because it turns out to be henceforth possible to decipher the entirety of the capitalist system in terms of subjectivity. Wherever this system holds sway, the more forcefully it is caught in its nets, and kidnapped on behalf of its immediate interests. For "*just like the social machines that can be arrayed under the general heading of collective facilities, so the technological machines of information and communication operate at the heart of human subjectivity*[2]". We must thus learn to "*seize, enhance and reinvent*" subjectivity, for otherwise we shall see it transformed into a rigid collective apparatus at the exclusive service of the powers that be.

Status and operation of subjectivity
This declaration of the *de facto* naturalisation of human subjectivity is an input of paramount importance. Phenomenology wielded it as the unsurpassable symbol of reality, beyond which nothing can exist, whereas structuralism saw in it at times something superstitious, and at others the effect of an ideology.
Here Guattari offers a complex and dynamic reading, contrasting with the deification of the subject which is common currency in the phenomenological vulgate, but just as impervious to the fossilisation being brought about by the structuralists, by placing it at the crossroads of the interplay of signifiers. We might say that Guattari's method consists in *bringing to boil* the structures fixed

by Lacan, Althusser and Lévi-Strauss: by replacing the static order by structural analyses, and the "slow movements" of Braudelian history by the novel, dynamic and undulatory linkages which matter takes on when it is reorganised by the effect of heat. Guattari's subjectivity is determined by a chaotic order, and no longer, as it was the case for the structuralists, by the quest for cosmoses hidden beneath everyday institutions. "*A certain balance still has to be found between structuralist discoveries, which are certainly considerable, and their pragmatic management, so as not to remotely founder in social post-modern abandonism*[3]".

This balance only comes about provided that the socius is observed at its proper temperature, at the heat of inter-human relationships, and not artificially "cooled", the better to single out the structures… This chaotic urgency gives rise to a certain number of operations. The first consists in unsticking the subjectivity of the subject, and doing away with the bonds that make it the natural attribute of this latter. So a mapping of it has to be drawn which spills considerably beyond the limits of the individual. But it is by extending the territory of the subjective to the regulatory impersonal machinery of sociability that Guattari can call on its "re-singularization", going beyond the traditional notion of *ideology*. Only a mastery of the "collective agencies" of subjectivity makes it possible to invent particular agencies. Real individuation proceeds by way of the invention of eco-mental recycling devices, just as the demonstration of economic alienation by Marx enables him to work on an emancipation of man within the world of labour. All Guattari does is indicate the degree to which subjectivity is alienated and dependent on a mental superstructure, and point to liberation possibilities.

This Marxist backdrop turns out to be readable even in the terms whereby Guattari defines subjectivity: "*All the conditions making it possible for individual and/or collective agencies to be in a position to emerge as sui-referential existential Territory, adjacent to or in a relation of delimitation with an otherness that is itself subjective[4]*". Otherwise put, subjectivity can only be defined by the presence of a second subjectivity. It does not form a "territory" except on the basis of the other territories it comes across; as an evolving formation, it is modelled on the difference which forms it itself, on the principle of otherness. It is in this plural, polyphonic definition of subjectivity that we find the perspective tremor that Guattari inflicts on philosophical economy. Subjectivity, he explains, cannot exist in an independent way, and in no case can it ground the existence of the subject. It only exists in the pairing mode: association with "*human groups, socio-economic machines, informational machines[5]*". Involved here is decisive, dazzling intuition. If the force of Marx's impact, in his *Theses on Feuerbach*, consisted in defining the crux of man as "the set of social relations", Guattari, for his part, defined subjectivity as the set of relations that are created between the individual and the vehicles of subjectivity he comes across, be they individual or collective, human or inhuman. This is a decisive breakthrough: the essence of the subjectivity of the subject was sought, and we find it, permanently off-centre, caught in "a-significant semiotic systems"... Here, Guattari shows himself to be still reliant on the world of structuralist references. Just as in the Lévi-Strauss forest, the signifier reigns supreme in Guattari's "machine-like subconscious"[6]. The "production of collective subjectivity" provides as much by the score, serving to construct "minimum territories" with which the individual can identify. What are the fluid signifiers that make up the production of subjectivity? First and foremost, the cultural environment ("family, education, environment, religion, art, sport"); then, cultural consumerism ("*things made by the media and film industry, etc.*"), ideological gadgets, spare parts of the subjective machinery... And last of all the set of informational machinery, which forms the a-semiological, a-linguistic chord of contemporary subjectivity, by "*operating in tandem with or independently of the fact that they produce meanings*". The process of singularisation consists, as it happens, in incorporating these signifiers in personal "existential territories", as tools helping to invent new relations "*to the body, to fantasy, to time passing, to the 'mysteries' of life and death*", and helping, too, to withstand the uniformization of thinking and behaving[7]. From this angle, social productions must be put through the sieve of a "*mental ecosophy*". Individual subjectivity is thus formed from the processing of the products of this machinery: as the outcome of *dissensus*, of gaps and differences, of alienating operations, it cannot be separated from all the other social relations, just like problems connected with the environment cannot be detached from all other production relations. This determination to handle existence like a network of interdependent factors, stemming from a unifying ecology, defines Guattari's relationship with the art thing: it is just one field of sensibility among others, associated with a global system. His thinking on ecology also led Guattari to become aware, before most people in the "aesthetics trade", of the obsolescence of the Romantic models still in force when it comes to describing modern art. Guattari's version of subjectivity thus provides aesthetics with an operational paradigm, which is in return legitimised by the practice of artists over the past three decades.

Subjectivization units

If Kant admitted landscapes and all natural forms in the field of applied aesthetics, we know that Hegel reined in this domain by reducing it exclusively to that specific class of objects formed by works of the mind. Romantic aesthetics, from which we may very well not have really emerged[8], postulates that the work of art, as a product of human subjectivity, expresses the mental world of a subject. During the 20th century, many theories discussed this Romantic version of creation, but without ever totally toppling its foundations. Let us mention the work of Marcel Duchamp, whose "ready-mades" reduced the author's own action or interference to merely selecting a mass-produced object and incorporating it in a personal linguistic system, thus redefining the artist's role in terms of responsibility towards the real. Or, alternatively, the generalised aesthetics of Roger Caillois, who put forms produced by accident, growth and mould on the same footing as those originating from a project[9]. Guattari's theses may head in the same direction, by refusing the Romantic idea of genius and depicting the artist as an operator of meaning, rather than a pure "creator" relying on crypto-divine inspiration, but they do not tally with those structuralist anthems about the "death of the author". For Guattari, a phoney problem is involved here. It is the processes of subjectivity production which need redefining with a view to their collectivisation. Because the individual does not have a monopoly on subjectivity, the model of the Author and his alleged disappearance are of no importance: "*Devices for producing subjectivity may exist in the scale of megalopolis as well as on the scale of an individual's linguistic games[10]*". The Romantic contrast between individual and society, which informs artistic role-playing and its mercantile system, has become truly null and void. Only a "transversalist" conception of creative operations, lessening the figure of the author in favour of that of the artist-cum operator, may describe the "mutation" under way: Duchamp, Rauschenberg, Beuys and Warhol all constructed their work on a system of exchanges with social movements, unhinging the mental "ivory tower" myth allocated to the artist by the Romantic ideology. It is not haphazard if the gradual dematerialization of the artwork, throughout the 20th century, came with an upsurge of the work within the sphere of work. The signature, which seals into the artistic economy the exchange mechanisms of subjectivity (an exclusive form of its distribution, turning it into a commodity), implies a loss of "polyphony", of that rough form of subjectivity represented by many-voiceness, in favour of a sterilising, reifying fragmentation. In *Chaosmosis*, in order to lament its loss, Guattari refers to a practice current in archaic societies which consists in giving a large number of proper names to one and the same individual.

Polyphony is nevertheless restored at another level, in these sets of subjectivization which bind heterogeneous arenas together. These blocks, "individual – group – machine – multiple exchanges[11]" which "*offer a person the possibility of getting back together as an existential corporeity, and becoming particular once again*" in the framework of a psychoanalytical therapy. Suffice it to accept the fact that subjectivity does not stem from any homogeneity. On the contrary, it develops it by cuts, segmenting and dismembering the illusory units of psychic life. "*It is not familiar with any predominant agency of determination steering other agencies in accordance with an unambiguous causality[12].*" When applied to artistic practices, this fact causes the total collapse of the notion of style. Endowed with the authority of the signature, the artist is usually introduced as the conductor of manual and mental faculties coiled around a single principle, its *style*. The modern, western artist is defined, first and foremost, as a subject whose signature acts as a "unifier of states of consciousness", producing a calculated muddle between subjectivity and style. But can we still talk in terms of the creative subject, the author and his mastery, when the "components of subjectivization", which "each work more or less on their own behalf[13]", only appear unified by the effect of a consensual illusion, the accredited guardians of which are signature and style, guarantors of the goods?

The Guattari subject is made up of independent plates, linking up with different pairings drifting towards heterogeneous fields of subjectivisation. The "Integrated World Capitalism" [IWC] described by Guattari only cares about the "existential territories" which it is art's mission to produce. Through the exclusive enhancement of the signature, a factor of behavioural homogenisation and reification, it can carry on in its role, i.e. transforming these territories into products. Otherwise put, wherever art proposes "life possibilities", IWC presents us with the *bill*. And what if real style, as Deleuze and Guattari write, were not the repetition of reified "making" but the "movement of thought"? Guattari contrasts the homogenisation and standardisation of types of subjectivity with the need to involve the being in "*heterogenetic processes*". This is the primary principle of mental ecosophy: articulating particular worlds and rare life forms; cultivating *per se* differentness, before *moving it* over into the social. The whole Guattari argument proceeds from this preliminary, inner modelling of social relations. Nothing is possible without a far-reaching ecological transformation of subjectivities, without an awareness of the various forms of founding interdependence of subjectivity. As such, it links up most of the century's avant-gardes, which called for a joint transformation of attitudes and social structures. Dadaism, Surrealism, and the Situationists, all thus tried to promote a total revolution, postulating that nothing could change in the infrastructure (the devices of production) if the superstructure (ideology) were not likewise far-reachingly refashioned. Guattari's plea for the "Three Ecologies" (environmental, social, and mental) under the aegis of an "aesthetic paradigm" likely to link up the various human claims and challenges, thus lies in the mainstream of modern artistic utopias.

The aesthetic paradigm

The critique of scientistic paradigm
In Guattari's "schizoanalytical" world, aesthetics has a place all of its own. It represents a "paradigm", a flexible agency capable of operating on several levels and on differing planes of knowledge. And, first and foremost, as the pedestal that enables it to propound its "ecosophy"; as a subjectivity-producing model; as an instrument used for enriching psychiatric and psychoanalytical practice. Guattari calls upon aesthetics to offset the hegemony of the "scientistic superego", which lays down

analytical practices in formulae. What he has against the "psy people" is the way they turn towards the past by manipulating Freudian and Lacanian concepts as so many insurmountable certainties. The subconscious itself is likened to an "*Institution, a collective amenity*"... Permanent revolution in method? "*The same should go* [...] *for painting and literature, areas within which the task of each concrete performance is to evolve, innovate, and usher in forward-looking openings, without their authors managing to lay claim to guaranteed theoretical foundations or the authority of a group, school, conservatory or academy*[14]". The only thing that matters is the "Work in progress". Thought originates from an art, which is not synonymous with rhetoric... So it should come as no surprise to read the definition given by Deleuze/Guattari to philosophy, "*the art of forming, inventing, and manufacturing concepts*[15]".

In a more general way, it was Guattari's intent to reshape the whole of science and technology based on an "aesthetic paradigm". "*My intention consists in conveying the human sciences and the social sciences from scientistic paradigms to ethical-aesthetic paradigms*", he explains. An intent that is akin to a form of scientific scepticism. For him, theories and concepts merely have the value of "models of subjectivization", *inter alia*, and no certainty is irrevocable. The primary criterion of scientificity, as stated by Popper, is falsifiability, is it not? According to Guattari, the aesthetic paradigm is called upon to contaminate every chord of discourse, and inoculate the venom of creative uncertainty and outrageous invention in every field of knowledge. Denial of claimed scientific "neutrality": "*what will henceforth be on the agenda is the clearance of 'futuristic' and 'constructivist' fields of virtuality*[16]". Portrait of the psychoanalyst as an artist: "*just as an artist borrows from his precursors and his contemporaries the features that suit him, so I invite those who read me to freely accept and reject my concepts*[17]".

Ritournelle, symptom and work

Like Nietzsche's aesthetics, from which Guattari's broadly originate, the latter only considers the creator's viewpoint. In it there is no sign of considerations to do with aesthetic reception, apart from those pages dealing with the notion of "ritournelle". It takes for example the fact of looking at television. For switching on the TV set is to expose "your feeling of personal identity" to temporary break-up. The TV viewer thus exists at the crossroads of several subjective nodes: the "perceptual fascination" caused by electronic image scanning; the "capture" obtained by narrative content, enlivened by perceptive "parasites" happening in the room, the telephone, for example; and lastly, the "world of fantasies" aroused by the programme, perceived as an "existential motif" working like an "attractor" within the "perceptible and significational chaos".

Plural subjectivity here is "ritournellized", "caught" by what it looks at, a prelude to the formation of an "existential territory". Here again, contemplation of form comes across not as any old kind of "suspension of the will" (Schopenhauer), but rather as a thermodynamic process, a phenomenon of condensation and accumulation of psychic energy on a "motif", with a view to action. Art fixes energy, and "ritournellizes" it, diverting it from everyday life: a matter of repercussion and ricochet.. As a pure *"clash between a will and a material[18]"*, art, for Guattari, might be compared with the thoroughly Nietzschean activity that consists in outlining *texts* in the *chaos* of the world. In other words, in the act of "interpreting and assessing"... The "existential motifs" offered for aesthetic contemplation, in a broad sense, catch the different components of subjectivity and guide them. Art is the thing upon and around which subjectivity can reform itself, the way several light spots are brought together to form a beam, and light up a single point. The opposite of this condensation, for which art provides the most conclusive example, is neurosis, in which the "ritournelle", hallmarked by fluidity, "hardens" into obsession; but psychosis, too, which makes the personality implode by making the "partial components" leave subjectivity "in hallucinatory, delirious lines[19]"… Which suggests to us that the *object* itself is neurotic: unlike the fluidity of "ritournellization", whose successive crystallisations bounce on supple partial objects, neurosis "hardens" whatever it touches. Integrated capitalism, which turns existential territories into goods and shunts subjective energy towards products, thus functions in neurotic mode. It produces an "immense void in subjectivity", a "machine-like solitude[20]", rushing into spaces left vacant by the desertification of direct trading areas. A void which can only be filled by drawing up a new contract with the inhuman, i.e. the machine.

Guattari's thinking is organised around an analytical perspective, the cure for which forms the distant horizon. Invariably, the method of partial healing emerges to re-form the shattered picture of forms of subjectivization. Art is never that far removed from the symptom, but does not overlap with it. This latter "*operates like an existential ritournelle from the moment when it is repeated*", when the ritournelle "*is embodied in a 'hardened' representation, for example, an obsessive ritual*". But if the analogy between the sick patient's assumption of independence and artistic creation is at times pushed very far, Guattari fights shy of "*likening psychosis to a work of art, and the psychoanalyst to an artist*"… Except that both deal with the same subjective material, which must be brought forward in order to "heal" the disastrous effects of homogenisation, that violence wielded by the capitalist system towards the individual; suppression of forms of dissent and disagreement that can only be founded by his subjectivity. In any event, art and psychic life are interwoven in the same agencies. Guattari only describes art in immaterial terms the better to materialise the mechanisms of the *psyche*. In analysis as in artistic activity, "*time stops being suffered; it is worked, oriented, as the object of qualificative changes*". If the analyst's role consists in "*creating mutant foci of subjectivization*", the formula might easily be applied to artists.

The work of art as partial object
The work of art is only of interest to Guattari insomuch as it is not
a matter of a "passively representative image", otherwise put, a
product. The work gives a material quality to existential territories,
within which the image takes on the role of *subjectivization vector*
or "shifter", capable of deterring our perception before "hooking it
up again" to other possibilities: that of an *"operator of junctions in
subjectivity"*. Here again, the work of art cannot claim anything
exclusive, even if it offers the model of that "pathic knowledge"
which is the particular feature of aesthetics, that "non-discursive
experience of the time span"... This type of knowledge is only
possible provided that we do not see mere delight in the
contemplation of the artwork. Guattari prowls in the vicinity of
Nietzsche, transposing the vitalism of the German philosopher ("A
problem that bestirs us to exceed ourselves is beautiful") into the
psycho-ecological area of vocabulary for which he has a soft spot.
In aesthetic contemplation he thus sees a process of
"subjectivization transfer". Borrowed from Mikhail Bakhtine, this
concept earmarks the moment when the "matter of expression"
becomes "formally creative"[21], a split-second in the telltale passage
between author and beholder.
Here, Guattari's postulates turn out to be very akin to those uttered
by Marcel Duchamp in his famous 1954 Houston lecture on "the
creative process"[22]: the beholder is the joint creator of the work,
venturing into the mysteries of creation by way of the "coefficient
of art", which is the "difference between what [the artist] had
planned to make and what he did". Duchamp described this
phenomenon in terms not unlike those of psychoanalysis: it is
indeed a question of a "transfer" of which "the artist is in no way
aware", and the reaction of the beholder in front of the work occurs
in a kind of "aesthetic osmosis which takes place through the inert
matter: colour, piano, marble, etc." This *transitional* theory of the
work of art was taken up by Guattari, who turned it into the
pedestal for his own hunches about the fluid nature of subjectivity,

whose component parts operate, as we have seen, by temporarily *clinging* to heterogeneous "existential territories". The work of art doesn't halt the eye. It's the spellbinding, para-hypnotic process of the aesthetic way of looking that crystallises around it the different ingredients of subjectivity, and redistributes them towards new vanishing points. The work is the opposite of the *buffer* defined by classical aesthetic perception, exercised on finished objects and closed entities. This aesthetic fluidity cannot be detached from a questioning addressed at the work's independence. Guattari defined this latter as a *"partial object"*, which derives advantage solely from a *"relative subjective autonomization"*, like object *a* in the Lacanian subconscious[23]. Here, the aesthetic object acquires the status of a "partial enunciator", whose assumption of autonomy makes it possible to *"foster new fields of reference"*. This definition embraces the development of art forms in a very fruitful way: the theory of the aesthetic *partial object* as "semiotic segment" separate from collective subjective production so as to start *"working on its own behalf"* perfectly describes the most widespread artistic production methods today: *sampling* of pictures and data, recycling now socialised and historicized forms, invention of collective identities... Such are the procedures of present-day art, stemming from a hyper-inflational system of imagery. These strategies for partial objects incorporate the work in the *continuum* of a device of existence, instead of endowing it with the traditional independence of the masterpiece in the system of conceptual mastery. These works are no longer paintings, sculptures or installations, all terms corresponding with categories of mastery and types of products, but simple *surfaces*, *volumes* and *devices*, which are dovetailed within strategies of existence. Here we are bordering on the limits of the definition of artistic activity proposed by Deleuze and Guattari in *What is Philosophy*: *"knowledge of the world through percepts and affects"*... For how could the very idea of a partial object referring to a singularisation movement of the heterogeneous ingredients of subjectivity bring on an idea of *totality*: *"the partial enunciator"* that forms the work of art does not depend on a specific category of human activity, so how could it be limited to this particular arrangement suggested by the level of "affects" and "percepts"? To be fully an artwork, it must also put forward concepts necessary for the working of these affects and percepts, as part of a total experience of thought. For want of such, the categorisation fought against by function is inevitably reformed at the level of the materials that ground thought. So it would seem to be more sound, in the light of Guattari's writings themselves, to define art as *a construction of concepts with the help of percepts and affects, aimed at a knowledge of the world...*

For an artistic, ecosophic practice
The ecosophic fact consists in an ethical-cum-political articulation between the environment, the social and subjectivity. It is a question of re-forming a lost political territory, lost by being riven by the deterritorializing violence of "Integrated World Capitalism". *"By exacerbating the production of material and immaterial goods, to the detriment of the consistency of individual and collective existential Territories, the contemporary period has given rise to an immense void in subjectivity which is tending to become more and more absurd and without recourse[24]"*. And ecosophic practice, geared to ideas of globalness and interdependence, aims to re-form these existential territories based on operational methods of subjectivity hitherto painstakingly underplayed. Ecosophy may claim *"to replace the old ideologies which used to mistakenly divide the social, the private and the civil into sectors[25]"*. From this angle, art is still a valuable auxiliary, insofar as it provides a "plane of immanence"[26], at once highly organised and very "absorbent", for the exercise of subjectivity. All the more so because contemporary art has developed in the sense of a denial of the independence (and thus of the sectorization) given it by the formalist theories of "modernism", of which Clement Greenberg was the prime advocate.

Nowadays, art is not defined as a place that imports methods and concepts, a zone of forms of hybridisation. As one of the driving spirits behind the *Fluxus* movement, Robert Filliou said that art offers an immediate "right of asylum" to all deviant practices which cannot find their place in their natural bed. So many forceful works of the last three decades only arrived in the realm of art for the simple reason that they had reached a limit in other realms. Marcel Broodthaers thus found a way of carrying poetry on in imagery; and Joseph Beuys found a way of pursuing politics in form. Guattari seems to have recorded these shifts, this capacity of modern art to embrace the most varied of production systems. He readily criticises art as a specific activity, conducted by a particular corporate body. The experience of the clinic accounts for a lot in this astonishment in front of this fragmentation of knowledge, this "corporatist subjectivity" that is in the end quite recent, a corporatist subjectivity that leads us, for example, into a reflex of "sectorization", to "*aestheticize a cave art in which everything suggests that it had an essentially technological and cultural range*".

The exhibition *Primitivism in 20th Century Art*, recently held at the MoMA in New York, thus fetishizes "*formal, formalist and in the end rather superficial correlations*", between works that are wrenched out of their context, "*on the one hand tribal, ethnic and mythical, on the other cultural, historical and economic*". The root of artistic practice lies in the production of subjectivity; it matters little what the specific production method may be. But this activity nevertheless turns out to be determined by the *enunciative agency* chosen.

The behavioural economy of present-day art
"How do you render a school class as an artwork?", asks Guattari[27]... He thus poses the final problem of aesthetics, that of its use, and its possible injection into fabric rendered rigid by the capitalist economy. Everything conspires to make us think that

modernity has been constructed, from the late 19th century on, on the idea of "life as artwork". Based on Oscar Wilde's formula, modernity is the moment when "it is not art imitating life, but life imitating art"... Marx is headed in the same direction, by criticising the classical distinction between *Praxis* (the act of self-transformation) and *poiesis* (the necessary, servile action aimed at producing and transforming matter). Marx thought, on the contrary, that "praxis moves constantly into poiesis, and vice versa". Later on, Georges Bataille built his work on the critique of this "renunciation of existence in exchange for function" which grounds the capitalist economy. The three orders –science, fiction and action– shatter human existence by *calibrating* it on the basis of preordained categories[28]. Guattari's brand of ecosophy likewise posits the totality of existence as a precondition for the production of subjectivity. In it, this latter takes pride of place, the place earmarked by Marx for labour, and which Bataille gives to *inner experience*, in an effort involving the individual and collective re-formation of lost subjectivity. For "*the only acceptable end purpose of human activities*," writes Guattari, "*is the production of a subjectivity that is forever self-enriching its relationship with the world*[29]". A definition that ideally applies to the practices of contemporary artists: by creating and staging devices of existence including working methods and ways of being, instead of concrete objects which hitherto bounded the realm of art, they use time as a material. The form holds sway over the thing, and movements over categories. The production of gestures wins out over the production of material things. These days, beholders are prompted to cross the threshold of "catalyst-like time modules", rather than contemplate immanent objects closed in on their world of reference. The artist goes as far as to come across as a world of subjectivization on the move, like the mannequin of his own subjectivity. He thus becomes the terrain of special experiences and the synthetic principle of his work, a development that foreshadows the entire history of modernity. In this behavioural economy, the art object acquires a kind of deceptive aura, an agent of resistance to its commercial distribution and a mimetic parasite of the same.

In a mental world where the readymade represents a particular model, as a collective production (the mass-produced object) assumed and recycled in an auto-poietic visual device, Guattari's lines of thinking help us to consider the changes currently under way in present-day art. But this, however, was not the primary aim of their author, for whom aesthetics must above all else go hand in hand with societal changes, and inflect them... The poetic function, which consists in re-forming worlds of subjectivization, possibly would not have any meaning if it, too, were not able to help us to negotiate the *"ordeal of barbarity, mental implosion, and chaosmic spasm which are taking shape on the horizon, to turn them into riches and unforeseeable pleasures*[30]"...

* Chance is important, but only in relation to production. Once exhibited, the work leaves the world of contrivance, and everything in it stems from an interpretation.

1. Félix Guattari, *Chaosmosis: An ethicoaesthetic paradigm*, Indiana Press. I only refer to precise works when the sentences quoted refer to a development in the author. For example, some quotations will not be annotated, because their content refers to several passages or several books.

2. *Chaosmosis.*

3. *Chaosmosis.*

4. *Chaosmosis.*

5. Félix Guattari, *The three ecologies*, Athlone Press, 2001.

6. *L'inconscient machinique. Essai de schizoanalyse*, Recherches, Paris, 1979.

7. *The three ecologies.*

8. Marc Sherringham, *Introduction à la philosophie esthétique*, Editions Payot, Paris, 1993.

9. Roger Caillois, *Cohérences aventureuses*, Editions Idées-Gallimard.

10. *Chaosmosis.*

11. *Chaosmosis.*

12. *Chaosmosis.*

13. *The three ecologies.*

14. *The three ecologies.*
15. Deleuze/Guattari, *What is philosophy*, Verso, London, 1994.
16. *The three ecologies.*
17. *Chaosmosis.*
18. *Chaosmosis.* See also: Félix Guattari, *"Cracks in the Street"*, in Flash Art, no. 135, Summer 1987.
19. Chaosmosis.
20. Félix Guattari, *"Refonder les pratiques sociales"*, in Le Monde diplomatique, *"L'agonie de la culture"*, October 1993.
21. *Chaosmosis.*
22. Marcel Duchamp, *"Le processus créatif"*, in *Duchamp du signe*, Editions Flammarion, Paris.
23. *Chaosmosis.*
24. *The three ecologies.*
25. *Chaosmosis.*
26. *What is philosophy.*
27. *Chaosmosis.*
28. Georges Bataille, *"L'Apprenti sorcier"*, in Denis Hollier, *Le collège de sociologie*, Editions Idées-Gallimard.
29. *Chaosmosis.*
30. *Chaosmosis.*

GLOSSARY

Academicism
1. An attitude that involves clinging to the defunct signs and forms of one's day, and rendering them aesthetic.
2. Synonym: pompous (pompier).
"And why wouldn't he do something pompous, if it pays off?" (Samuel Beckett).

Aesthetics
An idea that sets humankind apart from other animal species.
In the end of the day, burying the dead, laughter, and suicide are just the corollaries of a deep-seated hunch, the hunch that life is an aesthetic, ritualised, shaped form.

Art
1. General term describing a set of objects presented as part of a narrative known as *art history*. This narrative draws up the critical genealogy and discusses the issues raised by these objects, by way of three sub-sets: *painting, sculpture, architecture*.
2. Nowadays, the word "art" seems to be no more than a semantic leftover of this narrative, whose more accurate definition would read as follows: Art is an activity consisting in producing relationships with the world with the help of signs, forms, actions and objects.

Art (The end of)
"The end of art" only exists in an idealistic view of history. We can nevertheless, and not without irony, borrow Hegel's formula whereby "art, for us, is a thing of the past", and turn it into a figure of style: let us remain open to what is happening in the present, which invariably exceeds, a priori, our capacities of understanding.

Artist
When Benjamin Buchloch referred to the conceptual and minimal generation of the 1960s, he defined the artist as a "scholar/philosopher/craftsman", who hands society "the objective results of his labour". For Buchloch, this figure was heir to that of the artist as "mediumic and transcendental subject", represented by Yves Klein, Lucio Fontana and Joseph Beuys. Recent developments in art merely modify Buchloch's hunch. Today's artist appears as an operator of signs, modelling production structures so as to provide significant doubles. An entrepreneur/politician/director. The most common denominator shared by all artists is that they *show* something. The act of showing suffices to define the artist, be it a representation or a designation.

Behaviour
1. Beside those two established genres, the history of things and the history of forms, we still need to come up with a history of artistic behaviour. It would be naïve to think that the history of art represents a *whole* capable of perennially replacing these three sub-groups. An artist's *microbiography* would point up the things he has achieved within his œuvre.
2. Artist, producer of time.
All totalitarian ideologies show a distinctive wish to control the time in which they exist. They replace the versatility of time invented by the individual by the fantasy of a central place where

it might be possible to acquire the overall meaning of society. Totalitarianism systematically tries to set up a form of temporal motionlessness, and rendering the time in which it exists uniform and collective, a fantasy of eternity aimed first and foremost at standardising and monitoring patterns of behaviour. Foucault thus rightly stressed the fact that the art of living clashed with "*all forms of fascism, be they already there or lurking*".

Co-existence criterion
All works of art produce a model of sociability, which transposes reality or might be conveyed in it. So there is a question we are entitled to ask in front of any aesthetic production: "Does this work permit me to enter into dialogue? Could I exist, and how, in the space it defines?" A form is more or less democratic. May I simply remind you, for the record, that the forms produced by the art of totalitarian regimes are peremptory and closed in on themselves (particularly through their stress on symmetry). Otherwise put, they do not give the viewer a chance to complement them.
(see: Relational (aesthetics)).

Context
In situ art is a form of artistic activity that encompasses the space in which it is on view. This consideration by the artist of the exhibition venue consisted, yesterday, in exploring its spatial and architectural configuration. A second possibility, prevalent in the art of the 1990s, consists in an investigation of the general context of the exhibition: its institutional structure, the socio-economic features encompassing it, and the people involved. This latter method calls for a great deal of subtlety: although such contextual studies have the merit of reminding us that the artistic doing does not drop out of the sky into a place unblemished by any ideology, it is nevertheless important to fit this investigation into a prospect that goes beyond the primary stage of sociology. It is not enough

to extract, mechanically, the social characteristics of the place where you exhibit (the art centre, the city, the region, the country...), to "reveal" whatever it may be. For some artists whose complicated thinking represents an architecture of meanings, no more nor less (Dan Asher, Daniel Buren, Jef Geys, Mark Dion), how many conceptual hacks are there who laboriously "associate", for their show in Montelimar, nougat production and unemployment figures? The mistake lies in thinking that the sense of an aesthetic fact lies *solely* in the context.

2. Art after criticism

Once art "overtook" philosophy (Joseph Kosuth), it nowadays goes beyond critical philosophy, where conceptual art has helped to spread the viewpoint. Doubt can be cast over the stance of the "critical" artist, when this position consists in judging the world as he were excluded from it by divine grace, and played no part in it. This idealistic attitude can be contrasted with Lacanian intuition that the unconscious is its own analyst. And Marx's idea that explains that real criticism is the criticism of reality that exists through criticism itself. For there is no mental place where the artist might exclude himself from the world he represents.

Critical materialism

The world is made up of random encounters (Lucretius, Hobbes, Marx, Althusser). Art, too, is made up of chaotic, chance meetings of signs and forms. Nowadays, it even creates spaces within which the encounter can occur. Present-day art does not present the outcome of a labour, it is the labour itself, or the labour-to-be.

Factitiousness

Art is not the world of suspended will (Schopenhauer), or of the disappearance of contingency (Sartre), but a space emptied of the *factitious*. It in no way clashes with authenticity (an absurd value where art is concerned) but replaces coherences, even phoney ones, with the illusory world of "truth". It is the bad lie that betrays the hack, whose at best touching sincerity inevitably ends up as a forked tongue.

Form
Structural unity imitating a world. Artistic practice involves creating a form capable of "lasting", bringing heterogeneous units together on a coherent level, in order to create a relationship to the world.

Gesture
Movement of the body revealing a psychological state or designed to express an idea. Gesturality means the set of requisite operations introduced by the production of artworks, from their manufacture to the production of peripheral signs (actions, events, anecdotes).

Image
Making a work involves the invention of a process of presentation. In this kind of process, the image is an act.

Inhabiting
Having imagined architecture and art of the future, the artist is now proposing solutions for inhabiting them. The contemporary form of modernity is ecological, haunted by the occupancy of forms and the use of images.

Modern
The ideals of modernity have not vanished, they have been adapted. So "the total work of art" comes about today in its spectacular version, emptied of its teleological content. Our civilisation makes up for the hyperspecialization of social functions by the progressive unity of leisure activities. It is thus possible to predict, without too much risk attaching thereto, that the aesthetic experience of the average late 20th century

individual might roughly resemble what early 20th century avant-gardes imagined. Between the interactive video disk, the CD-ROM, ever more multi-media-oriented games consoles, and the extreme sophistication of mass recreational venues, discotheques and theme parks, we are heading towards the condensation of leisure in unifying forms. Towards a compact art? Once CD-ROM and CD-I drives are available, which have enough autonomy, books, exhibitions and films will be in competition with a form of expression that is at once more comprehensive and more thought-restricting, circulating writing, imagery and sound in new forms.

Operational realism
Presentation of the functional sphere in an aesthetic arrangement. The work proposes a functional model and not a maquette. In other words, the concept of dimension does not come into it, just as in the digital image, whose proportions may vary depending on the size of the screen, which, unlike the frame, does not enclose works within a predetermined format, but rather renders virtuality material in x dimensions.

Ready-made
Artistic figure contemporary with the invention of film. The artist takes his camera-subjectivity into the real, defining himself as a cameraman; the museum plays the part of the film, he records. For the first time, with Duchamp, art no longer consists in translating the real with the help of signs, but in presenting this same real as it is (Duchamp, the Lumière brothers...)

Relational (aesthetics)
Aesthetic theory consisting in judging artworks on the basis of the inter-human relations which they represent, produce or prompt. (See: co-existence criterion).

Relational (art)
A set of artistic practices which take as their theoretical and practical point of departure the whole of human relations and their social context, rather than an independent and private space.

Semionaut
The contemporary artist is a *semionaut*, he invents trajectories between signs.

Society of extras
The society of the spectacle has been defined by Guy Debord as the historical moment when merchandise achieved "the total occupation of social life", capital having reached "such a degree of accumulation" that it was turned into imagery. Today, we are in the further stage of spectacular development: the individual has shifted from a passive and purely repetitive status to the minimum activity dictated to him by market forces. So television consumption is shrinking in favour of video games; thus the spectacular hierarchy encourages "empty monads", i.e. programmeless models and politicians; thus everyone sees themselves summoned to be famous for fifteen minutes, using a TV game, street poll or news item as go-between. This is the reign of "Infamous Man", whom Michel Foucault defined as the anonymous and "ordinary" individual suddenly put in the glare of media spotlights. Here we are summoned to turn into *extras* of the spectacle, having been regarded as its consumers. This switch can be historically explained: since the surrender of the Soviet bloc, there are no obstacles on capitalism's path to empire. It has a total hold of the social arena, so it can permit itself to stir individuals to frolic about in the free and open spaces that it has staked out. So, after the consumer society, we can see the dawning of the society of extras where the individual develops as a part-time stand-in for freedom, signer and sealer of the public place.

Style

The movement of a work, its trajectory. "The style of a thought is its movement" (Gilles Deleuze and Félix Guattari).

Trailer

Having been an event per se (classical painting), then the graphic recording of an event (the work of Jackson Pollock, with photographic documents describing a performance or an action), today's work of art often assumes the role of a trailer for a forthcoming event, or an event that is put off forever.

INDEX

Acconci (Vito) 77
Adorno 76
Alberti 27
Alexander the Great 27
Althusser (Louis) 13, 15, 18, 24, 66, 90, 110
ARC 36, 37
Armaly (Fareed) 34
Bakhtine (Mikhail) 99
Balthus 86
Barry (Robert) 29
Basilico (Stefano) 33
Bataille (Georges) 44, 81, 103, 105
Beecroft (Vanessa) 8, 39, 48, 76
Ben 38
Benjamin (Walter) 60, 74, 78
Beuys (Joseph) 40, 70, 93, 102, 108
Bijl (Guillaume) 37
Blair (Dike) 39
Boetti (Alighiero) 68
Buchloch (Benjamin) 108
Boltanski (Christian) 29, 64
Bond (Henry) 36, 37, 46, 70, 74
Bourdieu (Pierre) 22, 26, 40

Brecht (George) 30, 70
Brinch (Jes) 8
Broodthaers (Marcel) 72, 73, 78, 102
Bulloch (Angela) 31, 58, 75
Burden (Chris) 19
Buren (Daniel) 20, 110
Caillois (Roger) 93, 104
Calle (Sophie) 30
Capc 36
Castoriadis (Cornélius) 54, 64
Cattelan (Maurizio) 8, 14, 33, 40
Certeau (Michel de) 14, 24
Cézanne (Paul) 20
Clegg & Guttman 34, 35
Clert Gallery (Iris) 37
Dada 12
Damisch (Hubert) 18, 24, 48
Daney (Serge) 21, 23, 24, 69, 75, 77, 78
Dante (Joe) 69
Danto (Arthur) 63
De Duve (Thierry) 24
Debord (Guy) 9, 19, 85, 113
Degas (Edgar) 67
Delacroix (Eugène) 19, 26
Deleuze (Gilles) 13, 20, 74, 87, 95, 96, 100, 105, 114
Deller (Jeremy) 30
Devautour 27
Dimitrijevic (Braco) 30
Dion (Mark) 35, 72, 110
Donatello 63
Donegan (Cheryl) 75
Duchamp (Marcel) 19, 25, 26, 29, 41, 44, 92, 93, 99, 105, 112
Durand (Gilbert) 45
Duyckaerts (Eric) 32

El Greco 63
Epicurus 19
Fairhurst (Angus) 32
Fend (Peter) 35, 37
Filliou (Robert) 30, 102
Fluxus 25, 46, 102
Foucault (Michel) 50, 109, 113
Frankfurt school 31
Fraser (Andrea) 32
Fried (Michael) 59, 64
General Idea 61
Gillick (Liam) 30, 32, 36, 37, 47, 48, 51
Godard (Jean-Luc) 26
Gombrowicz (Witold) 21, 22
Gonzalez-Foerster (Dominique) 30, 33, 34, 36, 48, 51, 52, 72
Gonzalez-Torres (Felix) 38, 39, 49, 50, 51, 52, 53, 54, 55,
    56, 58, 59, 63, 72
Gordon (Douglas) 32, 48, 51, 70, 73
Graham (Dan) 20, 46, 78
Greenberg (Clement) 67, 101
Guattari (Félix) 10, 20, 31, 40, 80, 86, 87, 88, 89, 90, 91, 92,
    93, 94, 95, 96, 97, 98, 99, 100, 101, 102, 103, 104, 105, 114
Haaning (Jens) 17, 77
Hempel (Lothar) 76
Hickey (Dave) 45, 62, 63, 64
Hill (Christine) 8, 36
Hirakawa (Noritoshi) 8, 34
Hirst (Damien) 39, 40
Höller (Carsten) 8, 36, 40, 58, 70, 73, 76, 82
Holzer (Jenny) 43
Huber Gallery (Pierre) 34
Huyghe (Pierre) 8, 30, 32, 40, 58, 70, 71, 74, 77
Hybert (Fabrice) 37, 72, 76
Ingold Airlines 35

Johns (Jasper) 46
Joisten (Bernard) 72, 73
Joseph (Pierre) 30, 38, 39, 72, 73, 76
Kant 92
Kawara (On) 30
Kelley (Mike) 44, 77
Kilimnik (Karen) 30
Kinmont (Ben) 31, 58
Klein (Yves) 37, 48, 108
Koons (Jeff) 43, 48
Kostabi (Mark) 35
Kosuth (Joseph) 52, 110
Kraftwerk 31
Kudo (Tetsumi) 44
La Borde 86
Lacan 90
Lambert (Alix) 34
Land (Peter) 46, 76
Landers (Sean) 75
Larner (Liz) 38
Latham (John) 35
Le Corbusier 35
Lecoq (Yves) 34
Leonardo da Vinci 27
Lévi-Strauss 90, 91
Lévinas (Emmanuel) 23, 24
LeWitt (Sol) 52
Lucretius 19, 110
Lyotard (Jean-François) 13, 24
MacCarthy (Paul) 77
Maffesoli (Michel) 15, 24, 64
Manetas (Miltos) 47, 74
Marx (Karl) 16, 42, 81, 90, 103
Matta-Clark (Gordon) 20, 30, 44, 46

Maubrie (Gabrielle) 33
McCaslin (Matthew) 38
Medeiros (Maria de) 34
Mondrian (Piet) 12
Monet (Claude) 67
Napoleon 27
New Realists 46
Nietzsche 69, 88, 97, 99
Orozco (Gabriel) 17, 58
Panamarenko 35
Pardo (Jorge) 47, 51, 52
Parreno (Philippe) 7, 30, 32, 34, 38, 51, 54, 70, 72, 73, 74,
    76, 78, 82
Perrin (Philippe) 38
Perrotin (Emmanuel) 33
Peterman (Dan) 35
Plenge Jacobsen (Henrik) 8
Pollock (Jackson) 41, 48, 79, 114
Popper 96
Premiata Ditta 34, 35, 75
Prince (Richard) 43
Proudhon 12
Ramo Nash Club 27, 73
Rauschenberg (Robert) 46, 93
Redon (Odilon) 28
Rhoades(Jason) 72
Rosen Gallery (Andrea) 38
Rothko (Mark) 79
Rousseau (Jean-Jacques) 15
Ruppersberg (Allen) 73
Samore (Sam) 33
Scher (Julia) 37
Schipper (Esther) 33, 39
Schopenhauer 97, 110

Schwitters (Kurt) 19
Serra (Richard) 52
Servaas Inc 35
Seurat (Georges) 28
Situationist International 12, 19
Situationists 12, 95
Smithson (Robert) 44, 46
Sonnabend (Ileana) 33
Spoerri (Daniel) 30
Starr (Georgina) 31
Surrealism 12, 95
Thek (Paul) 44
Thomas (Philippe) 36
Tiravanija (Rirkrit) 25, 30, 32, 48, 51, 54, 70, 75, 82, 83
Tobier (Lincoln) 32, 58
Todorov (Tzvetan) 23, 24
Tolstoy 27
Troncy (Eric) 80
Vaisman (Meyer) 40
Van de Steeg (Niek) 35, 37
Vernoux (Marion) 38
Walter (Franz Erhard) 70
Warhol (Andy) 20, 42, 74, 93
Wearing (Gillian) 46, 75
Willats (Stephen) 30
Zittel (Andrea) 58
Zobernig (Heimo) 32

CONTENTS

7   **Foreword**

11   **Relational Form**
11   *Contemporary artistic practice and its cultural plan*
14   *Artwork as social interstice*
18   *Relational aesthetics and random materialism*
21   *Form and others' gaze*

25   **Art of the 1990s**
25   ***Participation and Transitivity***
29   ***Typology***
29   *Connections and meetings*
30   *Convivialities and encounters*
33   *Collaborations and contracts*
35   *Professional relations: clienteles*
37   *How to occupy a gallery*

41   **Space-time exchange factors**
41   *Artworks and exchanges*
43   *The subject of the artwork*
46   *Space-time factors in 1990s' art*

49   **Joint presence and availability:**
      The theoretical legacy of Felix Gonzalez-Torres
50   *Homosexuality as a paradigm of cohabitation*
53   *Contemporary forms of the monument*
56   *The criterion of co-existence (works and individuals)*
58   *The aura of artworks has shifted towards their public*
62   *Beauty as a solution?*

65   **Screen relations**
65   *Today's art and its technological models*
66   *Art and goods*
66   *The law of relocation*
68   *Technology as an ideological model*
      (from trace to programme)
71   *The camera and the exhibition*
71   *The exhibition-set*
74   *Extras*
75   *Post VCR art*
75   *Rewind/play/fast forward*
77   *Towards a democratisation of viewpoints?*

79   **Towards a policy of forms**
79   *Cohabitations*
      Notes on some possible extensions of a relational aesthetics
79   *Visual systems*
80   *The image is a moment*
80   *What artists show*
80   *The boundaries of individual subjectivity*
81   *The engineering of intersubjectivity*
81   *An art with no effect?*
83   *The political development of forms*
84   *Rehabilitating experimentation*
84   *Relational aesthetics and constructed situations*

86   *The aesthetic paradigm*
        (Félix Guattari and art)
88   **Subjectivity pursued and produced**
88   *De-naturalising subjectivity*
89   *Status and operation of subjectivity*
92   *Subjectivization units*
95   **The aesthetic paradigm**
95   *The critique of scientistic paradigm*
97   *Ritournelle, symptom and work*
99   *The work of art as partial object*
101   *For an artistic-ecosophical practice*
102   *The behavioural economy of present-day art*

107   GLOSSARY

115   INDEX

Achevé d'imprimer sur rotative par l'Imprimerie Darantiere
à Dijon-Quetigny en janvier 2006

Dépôt légal : mars 2002 – N° d'impression : 25-1833

Imprimé en France